Major
Black
Religious
Leaders:
1755–1940

Major
Black
Religious
Leaders:
1755–1940

Henry J. Young

Abingdon
Nashville

Major Black Religious Leaders: 1755–1940

Copyright © 1977 by Abingdon

Library of Congress Cataloging in Publication Data

YOUNG, HENRY J 1943-
  Major Black religious leaders, 1755-1940.

  Includes bibliographical references.
  1. Afro-Americans—Religion—History. 2. Black theology—
History. I. Title.
BR563.N4Y68   299'.6   76-51731

ISBN 0-687-22913-8

Excerpt of "If We Must Die" from *Selected Poems of
Claude McKay* is reprinted with the permission of
Twayne Publishers, A Division of G. K. Hall & Co.,
Boston.

MANUFACTURED BY THE PARTHENON PRESS AT
NASHVILLE, TENNESSEE, UNITED STATES OF AMERICA

Dedicated to my wife

Aleta Joyce

Acknowledgments

I am indeed grateful for the assistance provided by the Atlanta University Center through a Spencer Foundation grant that made the research and writing of this book possible. I am also thankful for the assistance that I received from the Interdenominational Theological Center in Atlanta, which aided my research greatly.

Josephus R. Coan, professor emeritus of the Mission of the Church at the Interdenominational Theological Center, read the manuscript in the original and made many helpful suggestions. Jimmie F. Williams, administrative secretary to Quinland R. Gordon, dean of the Absalom Jones Theological Institute, made many helpful editorial corrections. She also assisted with the typing of the manuscript. In addition to her normal duties as my secretary, Eugenia P. Blair assisted me in this project by working as my Spencer Foundation clerical assistant. I am very appreciative to John Blair for facilitating this project by compiling information from countless articles and manuscripts. Cassandra E. Norman, assistant librarian at the Interdenominational Theological Center, was very helpful in directing me to several key sources. Honor J. Davenport, archivist at the Interdenominational Theological Center, made various rare books and manuscripts available to me. I am thankful for the assistance provided by the staffs of the Moorland-Spingarn Research Center, Howard University, the Fisk University Special Collection on Black Studies, the Library of Congress, the Rare Book

MAJOR BLACK RELIGIOUS LEADERS

Collection of the Boston Public Library, and all the libraries that make up the Atlanta University Center.

Special thanks to my wife, Aleta Joyce, who greatly aided the completion of this volume by working as my Spencer Foundation research assistant. I constantly discussed the scope, content, and goal of this book with her, and she made many necessary criticisms. During the writing of this book, she was a great source of encouragement and inspiration. She was also very understanding of the many hours that I had to spend confined to my study; for this I will always be grateful.

Henry James Young
Interdenominational Theological Center
Atlanta, Georgia

Contents

Introduction   13

Chapter I   Nathaniel Paul (1755?–1839)
    Early Life and Development   16
    Theology of Nathaniel Paul   16
        God and Slavery   16
        Sin   19
        Man and Eschatology   20
    Contribution   23

Chapter II   Richard Allen (1760–1831)
    Early Life and Conversion Experience   25
    The Independent Black Church   28
    Theology of Richard Allen   30
        God   30
        Man   32
        Eschatology and Ethics   34
    Contribution   38

Chapter III   David Walker (1785–1830)
    Early Life and Development   41
    Richard Allen and David Walker on the
        American Colonization Society   43
    Theology of David Walker   44
        God and Black Suffering   44
        Eschatology and Redemption   48
        Repentance   49
    Contribution   50

MAJOR BLACK RELIGIOUS LEADERS

Chapter IV Nat Turner (1800?–1831)
Early Life and Development   52
Theology of Nat Turner   53
Messianic Call   53
Liberation Theology   55
Contribution   58

Chapter V Daniel Alexander Payne (1811–1893)
Significant Events in the Early
Life of Payne   61
Theology of Daniel Payne   63
God, Providence, and Evil   63
Man   68
Eschatology   70
Contribution   71

Chapter VI James W. C. Pennington (1812–1871)
Early Life and Development   74
Theology of James Pennington   75
The Bible and Slavery   75
Ethics   77
Salvation   79
Man   80
Eschatology   81
Contribution   83

Chapter VII Henry Highland Garnet (1815–1882)
Brief Sketch of Garnet's Life   85
Black Unity   87
Critique of Slavery   89
Theology of Henry Highland Garnet   90
A Theology of Resistance   90
Sin and Repentance   93
Redemption   94
Contribution   96

CONTENTS

Chapter VIII   Samuel Ringgold Ward (1817–1878)
    Early Life and Development   *98*
    Antislavery   *99*
    Theology of Samuel Ward   *102*
       God   *102*
       Fugitive Slave Law, Ethics, and
         Eschatology   *104*
    Contribution   *107*

Chapter IX   Alexander Crummell (1819–1898)
    Early Life and Development   *110*
    Theology of Alexander Crummell   *113*
       God, Providence, and Evil   *113*
       Man, Ethics, and Eschatology   *119*
    Contribution   *125*

Chapter X   Edward Wilmot Blyden (1832–1912)
    Early Life and Development   *127*
    Christianity, Slavery, and Pan-Africanism   *129*
    Theology of Edward Blyden   *130*
       Providence and Pan-Africanism   *130*
       Man   *134*
       Eschatology   *136*
    Contribution   *137*

Chapter XI   Henry McNeal Turner (1834–1915)
    Early Life and Development   *140*
    Theology of Henry Turner   *142*
       God, Providence, and Evil   *142*
       Eschatology   *145*
       Man   *147*
    Contribution   *149*

Chapter XII   Marcus Garvey (1887–1940)
    Early Life and Development   *152*

Garvey and Africa   155
Theology of Marcus Garvey   157
    God   157
    Man and Providence   158
    Eschatology   160
Contribution   161

Conclusion   163
Notes   165

Introduction

By exposing oneself to the ideas and concepts of the black religious leaders discussed in this volume, it is my hope that the reader will be able to understand and appreciate more fully the black church, black religion, black theology, and the many contributions black religionists have made to the quest for black liberation. Each thinker perceived God, man, eschatology, liberation, providence, evil, and other theological motifs from a particular theological orientation; yet there is an organizing factor in their thought which creates an excellent case of unity in diversity. They all speak from a Christian context, and they interpret the theological motifs underlying the Christian faith in light of an organismic conception of reality. This is to say that they do not perceive reality as bifurcated and compartmentalized but as interconnected, interwoven, and interlocked. They do not separate spiritual liberation from physical liberation. They perceive spiritual liberation as a reality that is inextricably bound up with social phenomena. This means that the social, economic, and political dimensions of reality are understood by the thinkers discussed in this volume as interdependent. As we will discover, these thinkers view spirituality in terms of its function, as a phenomenon grounded in the transformation of society.

The eschatological perspective from Richard Allen to Marcus Garvey is primarily grounded in the flight of black Americans toward freedom and liberation in this life. However, their eschatology contains an acute aware-

13

ness of the vertical dimension of reality as well as the horizontal. They are calling for the complete eradication of slavery, oppression, man's inhumanity to man, injustice, sin, unrighteousness, and all forms of social evils that minimize man's actualization of his potentialities. Thus, in order for man to ascend to the heights of the realization of God's possibilities, he must be liberated both spiritually and physically. This can be referred to as a kind of realized eschatology. It is an expression of man's attempt to make the kingdom of God a living reality within the historical process. It does not negate the concern for heaven or an otherworldly eschatological hope, but the affirmation of heaven is not done by minimizing, negating, or repudiating the existential actualization of God's possibilities in this world.

Along with the above stated direction of this volume, another task is the attempt to speak to the pressing need to reinterpret the theological motifs underlying the black religious experience, to correct the many unwarranted distortions that have been made about black religionists, black religion, and the black church. Many historians, sociologists, anthropologists, and theologians have argued that black religion historically has not been focused on the transformation of social, political, and economic institutional structures but has been overly emotional and exclusively spiritualistic and heavenly-oriented. An example of this distortion is the statement made by Gunnar Myrdal in reference to black religion: "Negro frustration was sublimated into emotionalism, and Negro hopes were fixed on the afterworld." This view, in large measure, has given black religion a passive, submissive, escapist, and compensatory orientation. And, unfortunately, this distorted view has dominated the way in which scholarship has interpreted the black religious experience in America. It is hoped that on the basis of an examination of the motifs underlying the theological systems of the black religious leaders discussed in this volume the reader will be able to discover that, historically, black religion has been concerned with freedom, liberation, humanization, and the eradication of social evils in this world. Therefore, as opposed to being fixated exclusively with spirituality and heaven, the black church has been the vanguard of social, economic, and political activism within the black community.

Chapter I
Nathaniel Paul
1755?–1839

Early Life and Development

It was in Albany, New York, that Nathaniel Paul delivered his most famous antislavery discourse entitled "An Address Delivered on the Celebration of the Abolition of Slavery in the State of New York, July 5, 1827." This address enabled him to have a rightful place alongside the great antislavery advocates in American history. He was born around 1755 and at one time served as pastor of the African Baptist Church of Albany, New York. His early antislavery efforts made him a pioneer in the quest for black liberation and the ultimate redemption of mankind. He was one of the first to join the antislavery ranks and "was denouncing slavery years before Garrison, Phillips and Sumner appeared upon the scene."[1] After leaving the African Baptist Church of Albany, Paul expanded his antislavery efforts by traveling extensively through Canada and Europe lecturing and preaching.

Theology of Nathaniel Paul

God and Slavery

The reality of God as conceived by Nathaniel Paul can best be understood in light of his bitter protest against the

16

institution of slavery. He perceived God as a dynamic power immanent in the affairs of mankind. He did not think of God as a reality totally removed from the world and uninvolved in the historical process. This is not to mean, however, that he perceived the reality of God as totally dissolved into the world. He maintained the traditional view of God's transcendence and immanence. The transcendence of God is reflected in Paul's writings concerning heaven and life after death. It is also reflected in his assertion concerning the unrevealed mystery of God. At many points, Paul raised questions to God. These questions grew out of his existential religious situation, and they reflect an aspect of God's transcendence that Paul expressed as incomprehensible. He had difficulty reconciling God's intrinsic goodness, his justice, omnipotence, and righteousness with slavery.

He felt that slaves experienced "the most abject state of degraded misery" and were forced to experience and suffer the worst form of slavery, oppression, and man's inhumanity to man that human nature is capable of enduring. Reflecting on the many atrocities of slavery, Paul began to wonder whether it would have been better for those original Africans who were captured and forced onto the ships and brought to America to have died rather than to become slaves.[2] He believed that those who died on the slave ships en route to America were fortunate because they did not have to encounter the evils of slavery.

Why, Paul asked, did the mighty waters of the ocean sustain the ponderous and cruel misery of human bondage and captivity by which the slaves were forced to come to America? Why did the wind execute its office in making it possible for the slave ships to move onward to the still more dismal state of human bondage and misery? And, why didn't the gigantic waves of the ocean

17

overwhelm the slave ships? Then would they have slept sweetly in the bosom of the great deep and would have been hidden from the evils of slavery. Paul, therefore, moved to the core of pessimism and asked God, Why was it "that thou didst look on with the calm indifference of an unconcerned spectator, when thy holy law was violated, thy divine authority despised and a portion of thine own creatures reduced to a state of mere vassalage and misery?"[3] How did God answer Paul? How did God answer the enslaved black Americans? Paul raised the fundamental problem of evil. How can we reconcile human suffering, bondage, injustice, slavery, and unrighteousness with the intrinsic goodness, mercy, righteousness, and justice of God? Not only did the empirical reality of slavery go against the omnipotence and intrinsic goodness of God, but it also raised a serious question about the extent of God's involvement in the affairs of history. It becomes clear, at this point, that Paul's conception of God was grounded in hard-core empirical reality; it grew out of the social realities in which he found himself. In the midst of the pessimism of slavery, does Paul succumb to defeat, hopelessness, and despair? He found a way out of this pessimism in the manner in which he conceived of God's transcendence. The transcendence of God, for Paul, brings in a new dimension to existence; it overcomes, outruns, and goes beyond the pessimism of slavery, man's inhumanity to man, oppression, and evil. In this connection, Paul said that God answered in the following manner: "Be still, and know that I am God! clouds and darkness are round about me; yet righteousness and judgment are the habitation of my throne."[4]

Paul felt that God does his will and pleasure in the heavens above and the earth beneath. In the midst of the manifold presence of evil in the world it is legitimate to question the ways of God, but in doing so his objective essence should not be totally relegated to his activity in the world. Paul believed that in the midst of the evils of slavery, God's righteousness and judgment prevailed and remained sound. He also believed that God, in his omnipotence, possessed the capacity both to prevent and to eradicate slavery. What then does Paul do? He exonerates God in spite of slavery, oppression, and the manifold presence of evil in the world. He argues that God has the freedom to do his will in the transcendent realm of existence and in the immanent domain of his existence in the world. He concludes by saying that God brings good out of evil and causes the wrath of man to praise him and the remainder of the wrath of man God sustains.[5]

Sin

Nathaniel Paul's conception of sin, as his doctrine of God, was grounded in social phenomena. He thought of sin as disobedience to God and perceived the highest manifestation of this disobedience expressed in the institution of slavery. He thought of slavery as sinful in that it was contrary to the laws of God and was in violation of the rule of action by which the ethics of man is to be regulated toward his neighbor.[6] He categorized slavery as a cruel institution and as one of the most inhuman institutions ever to have been created by man. It was cruel, Paul said, because it forced black Americans from their native land and insisted that they fight for the liberties of the country in which they found themselves enslaved. In a sense black Americans built America with the sweat and endurance of their physical strength, and they found themselves, as Paul expressed, living in oppression, alienation, and captivity in their own land. He also felt that slavery was cruel and evil because it robbed black Americans of "every right, civil, political or religious, to which they are entitled by the American

19

Declaration of Independence."[7] Slavery, Paul continued, was a hateful monster, the worst evil of avarice and oppression.

He did not perceive God as responsible for the evils of slavery and oppression. It does, however, appear to be paradoxical to contend on the one hand that God is intrinsically good and all-powerful and on the other hand that he permitted black Americans to be enslaved. In an attempt to speak to this dilemma, Paul argued, "It was the gracious ordinance of Providence, both in the natural and moral world, that good should often arise out of evil."[8] The danger here, and Paul was aware of it, is to view evil as necessary for good to triumph. This condones evil, suffering, and man's inhumanity to man. It glorifies evil and makes all history necessary for the unfolding of God's plan and purpose for the world. Evil becomes a temporary negativity used by God to facilitate the ultimate victory of the good. The slaveholders employed this manner of thinking in attempting to indoctrinate the slaves into believing that they were predestined by God to be slaves.[9] But of course Paul rejected this notion of slavery's being preordained by God and argued that slavery was in contradiction to God's will and purpose for man. He did not believe that slavery was a necessary evil for black Americans to achieve freedom. He held this position in spite of his contention that good comes out of evil. He argued that blacks were going to achieve freedom and liberation in spite of the evils of slavery and oppression.

Man and Eschatology

Nathaniel Paul based his conception of man on the biblical doctrine of man. As his point of departure, Paul accepted the view of man found in Acts 17:26 which says God "hath made of one blood all nations of men for to dwell on all the face of the earth." Based on this passage, he realized that black Americans were as important in the eyes of God as white Americans. Therefore, he concluded, there are no inferior and superior races. In the eyes of God all men are significant. Paul believed that in creating man God just happened to have made some black and some white, but this difference in color, he declared, did not make either race superior or inferior to the other. He felt that black Americans did not have to feel sorry for themselves because God made them black; nor did they have to be ashamed of themselves. Paul believed that God has no respecter of persons or races.[10]

Paul accepted the biblical notion that God created perfect man and that the fall of man represented the origination of sin in the world. It set the stage for man's capacity and desire to enslave his fellowman. And as a result of the fall, man was ordered by God: "In the sweat of thy face shalt thou eat bread, till thou return unto the ground; for out of it wast thou taken: for dust thou art, and unto dust shalt thou return" (Gen. 3:19). But contrary to this sacred law of God, Paul argued, slavery forced black Americans to work with no remuneration, thereby enhancing the luxuries and wealth of the slaveholders.

He viewed black Americans as eschatological creatures—that is, they were moving toward God's goal and purpose for them. Paul's eschatology was not grounded in a notion of the end of history or with God's consummation of history eventuating in a kind of complete otherworldliness. To the contrary, he developed a realized eschatology. He looked and worked for the freedom and liberation of black Americans here in this world. He said, "We look forward with pleasing anticipation to that period when it shall no longer be said that in a land of freemen there are men in bondage." He realized that the progress of freedom was slow but nevertheless certain and inevitable. He felt that it was certain and

21

inevitable because God makes all men of the same blood and has no undue respecter of persons; therefore, it is not God's will for one race to enslave and oppress another. Since it is God's will that all men be free, Paul declared that slavery in the United States and throughout the world would ultimately be abolished. This anticipated total freedom and liberation of mankind within history, Paul believed, would materialize in spite of the strong opposition from the slaveholders. Regardless of what the United States and other slaveholding nations did to prevent the emancipation of slaves, Paul said, "But still I declare that slavery will be extinct; a universal and not a partial emancipation must take place; nor is the period far distant." He based this hope and affirmation on several things: the efforts of philanthropists in England to have slavery abolished in the West Indian islands, revolutions in South America, the catastrophy and redistribution of power in Haiti, the restless disposition of slaves and slaveholders in the southern states of America, and the irrevocable decrees of the almighty God.[11]

The eschatology of Nathaniel Paul geared itself toward optimism rather than pessimism. This is why he argued that emancipation was inevitable. He realized that the apparent paradox between God's intrinsic goodness, righteousness, justice, and omnipotence and the manifold presence of slavery and oppression was neither final nor ultimate. Since slavery and oppression were in direct contradiction to God's will and purpose, Paul knew that they would exhaust themselves and run out. It was this strong hope and faith that enabled him to continue to fight against slavery and oppression. He felt that he was not fighting a losing battle. He said that if he believed that slavery would always continue and that white people to the end of time would be permitted to enslave and oppress black people, he would disallow any allegiance or obligation he had to his fellowman, and he would deny the sovereignty and omnipotence of God's divine providence in the affairs of this life. He would ridicule the religion of the Savior of the world and treat as the worst of men the ministers of the everlasting gospel. He would consider his Bible a book of false and delusive fables and commit it to the flames. He would even go to the extent of confessing himself an atheist.[12] From this it is clear that Paul believed that God was directing history, not in the interest of perpetuating the institution of slavery and oppression, but in the interest of destroying it.

Contribution

Nathaniel Paul made a significant contribution to the history of theological thought in America. He was a pioneer in making theology existentially relevant for the freedom and liberation of man, both spiritually and physically. His theological presuppositions were undergirded by the social, political, economic, and educational structures of his day. His main concern was with the abolition of slavery and with the total development of black Americans. He conceived of God in a way that made his existence dynamically involved in the eradication of slavery. His eschatology was this-worldly and not otherworldly; he was concerned with the emancipation of black Americans and all oppressed people here on earth. He predicted that slavery would be abolished in America and throughout the world on the basis that it was in total opposition to the will of God. Being a churchman, Nathaniel Paul clearly set the stage for the black church to function historically as the vanguard of social, political, economic, educational, and religious activism within the black community. His theology and sense of ministry were concerned with the totality of man's existence. He did not separate spiritual liberation from physical liberation. He integrated the religious questions with the social questions. For him, spirituality was of no value apart from its capacity to liberate man into a genuine authentic human being and its capacity to lead man toward the transformation of the social, economic, political, and educational structures that oppress man.

Chapter II
Richard Allen
1760–1831

Early Life and Conversion Experience

On February 14, 1760, Richard Allen was born a slave to Benjamin Chew of Philadelphia. He was later sold to a slaveholder in Delaware state, near Dover. Allen lived with his new slaveholder, Stokeley, until he was twenty years old. He then was converted and began to preach the gospel. [1]

Allen's conversion was a significant experience in his development and outlook on life. It gave him a sense of recognition and acceptance by God, which meant a great deal to him. Prior to his conversion experience he described himself as poor, wretched, undone, without mercy, and lost. He felt unworthy to stand before God because of his sinful predicament. However, this humble feeling was the kind of attitude Allen felt was acceptable before God; Allen felt that God would transform this feeling of unworthiness into a feeling of worthiness and importance. That is why he believed that "God delighteth to hear the prayers of a poor sinner." [2]

Allen's conversion experience gave him the confidence and assurance that God was with him and that God cared about him. This experience gave him a sense of inner peace, inner freedom, regeneration, rebirth, individua-

25

tion, and a new level of consciousness.[3] It also gave him a new sense of selfhood, identity, and status. Since slaves were defined as property to be used and sold, Allen could not find authentic selfhood, identity, and meaningful status within the institution of slavery. But his experiential encounter with God broke all those shackles. He said that after his conversion experience his "chains flew off."[4] These chains were both intangible and tangible.

The psychological inferiorities, the intangible chains, Allen was victimized by as a result of slavery were broken as he affirmed himself in God as being somebody of importance and stature, in spite of the negativities of slavery. Allen was aware of the paradox between his inner freedom and the tangible chains of his physical bondage. He, therefore, after his conversion experience, sought to obtain his physical freedom.

Allen's physical freedom was made possible, because of the conversion experience of his slave master and because of Allen's ability to work and purchase his freedom. Allen had several religious services at his slave master's house. At one of these services, Freeborn Garrettson preached on the topic "Thou Art Weighed in the Balance and Art Found Wanting."[5] After this sermon, Allen's slave master converted and, as a result, felt dissatisfied with having slaves, because his conversion experience revealed to him that it was morally wrong. He then gave Allen the opportunity to work and purchase his freedom. This whole process raises an interesting question, which will be discussed after discussing the motive behind Allen's slave master's willingness to permit Allen to attend religious services when many slaveholders prevented their slaves from doing so.

Allen's slave master became convinced that religion made his slaves obedient, humble, passive, submissive, and excellent workers. Allen reported, "Our master said

26

he was convinced that religion made slaves better and not worse, and often boasted of his slaves for their honesty and industry." The opinion of many slaveholders on religion among slaves was summarized at a meeting of slaveholders in Charleston, South Carolina, during the antebellum period: "The deeper the piety of the slave, the more valuable is he in every sense of the word."[6] Slaveholders felt that, if properly taught, Christianity could not fail to render the slaves happier, more tranquil, docile, submissive, obedient, and committed.[7]

Slaveholders organized religious-instruction programs that attempted to indoctrinate the slaves into believing that they were predestined to be servants, that the institution of slavery had divine sanction, and that insolence was against both God and the master. The slaves were taught that servants must obey their masters—that is, if they were obedient to the divine command, God would give them eternal life in the hereafter; if they were not obedient, God would punish them in the hereafter. The slaves were taught that slavery was the fulfillment of God's providential plan. Benjamin Quarles reports that catechisms for the religious institution of slavery commonly consisted of such passages as:

> Q: Who gave you a master and a mistress?
> A: God gave them to me.
> Q: Who says that you must obey them?
> A: God says that I must.[8]

Frederick Douglass said that during his travels throughout the South, he observed that many slaves believed that "God required them to submit to slavery and to wear their chains with meekness and humility."[9] The majority of slaves, however, did not submit to slavery; they never accepted it, and every chance they could get, they resisted it. This constant resistance to slavery and

27

oppression contributed significantly to the emergence of the independent black church.

The Independent Black Church

The independent black church was born in protest to racism and discrimination. Richard Allen and a small group of blacks usually attended St. George Methodist Episcopal Church in Philadelphia without any serious resentment from the white members of that church. However, when the number of blacks attending St. George Methodist Episcopal Church increased significantly, Allen said that "they moved us from the seats we usually sat on, and placed us around the wall."[10] Not only were the blacks placed around the wall, but the sextons of the church attempted also to put the blacks in the gallery. This practice of segregating blacks from whites during service was not unique to St. George Methodist Episcopal Church; it was widespread during the antebellum period. There were, however, many occasions when blacks and whites worshiped together without large-scale discrimination. But in terms of the dominant trend, every effort was made on the part of the whites to segregate themselves from blacks during worship. The area reserved for blacks during worship was largely referred to as "the Negro Pew."[11] Blacks found themselves segregated in and alienated from the same churches that they contributed significantly to financially and in the physical construction. Allen said that blacks were turned out of St. George Methodist Episcopal Church just when they had committed themselves to building the gallery, laying new floors, and renovating the church.

This experience that Allen and his followers had at St. George made Allen realize that he was correct in his earlier effort and desire to erect an independent church for blacks. He saw this need before he and his followers were forced out of St. George Church. He expressed this desire and need before some of the leading black citizens of Philadelphia but experienced much opposition. There were only three blacks who united with him originally in the effort to start an independent black church; they were Absalom Jones, William White, and Dorus Ginnings. Allen and his three friends were members of St. George Church; Allen did not want to detach himself from Methodism or from the conference with which St. George was affiliated, but he wanted a place that blacks could call their own. He knew that in this independent church, blacks would have freedom of expression, freedom from white control, and a sense of integrity, dignity, and importance.

Allen and his band of blacks decided to leave St. George Church on Sunday morning immediately after prayer; the men walked out of the church, and the whites were plagued with them no more. This experience gave rise to the beginning of the African Methodist Episcopal Church in America.[12] Allen and his friends did not submit to the racism and discrimination of St. George Church; they resisted it and protested it.

After Allen and his group left St. George every effort was made by the Methodist connection to prevent them from starting an independent church. They were threatened with being disowned and turned out of the Methodist Conference. At this point, Allen felt determined to continue with the organization and establishment of the A.M.E. Church in spite of the persecution and opposition from the Methodist Conference. Allen was convinced that the A.M.E. Church had to be established because of the degrading and dehumanizing situation he and his friends experienced at St. George Church when they were dragged off their knees and treated worse than animals.[13]

Allen purchased an old frame building and officially opened it for worship in 1794; Bishop Asbury dedicated the church for Allen and his friends. Allen was ordained by Bishop Asbury as a deacon in 1799 and later became an elder. Blacks in neighboring cities, such as Baltimore, Wilmington, Attleboro, and Salem, followed Richard Allen's example in organizing and establishing independent A.M.E. churches. Absalom Jones originally started with Allen, but, because of disagreements, Jones organized the African Protestant Episcopal Church of St. Thomas, and Allen continued with the A.M.E. Church. In 1816 a general meeting was called in Philadelphia, and some of the independent black churches organized themselves under the name of the African Methodist Episcopal Church. Along with the purpose of becoming united as one body, the A.M.E. churches came to Philadelphia in 1816 to elect their first bishop. Daniel Coker was elected the first bishop of the A.M.E. Church; however, for several reasons he resigned the next day in favor of Richard Allen. Allen was then elected bishop and consecrated by ordained ministers.[14]

Theology of Richard Allen

God

Allen's conception of God was very much influenced by the social conditions of his day. He did not develop an abstract philosophical-theological conception of God detached from his everyday existential experiences. He conceived of God as being organically integrated and interwoven with all of life. For this reason, he did not make a disjunction between physical liberation and spiritual liberation. God, for him, was a part of both dimensions of life. Following this organic conception of God, Allen avoided making a gulf between God and man. On the one hand he thought of God as transcendent, sovereign, and omnipotent. And on the other hand he thought of God as being immanent and forever present with man. The biblical passage "Come unto me, all ye that labour and are heavy laden, and I will give you rest" (Matt. 11:28) gave Allen the awareness of the immanence of God. This helped Allen realize that God was a God at hand.[15] God, in this sense, becomes forever relevant to man's existential needs and desires.

Allen believed that God was always with him. This feeling of the interrelationship between God and man gave Allen the courage to oppose slavery, oppression, racism, injustice, sin, man's inhumanity to man—all forms of unrighteousness. He felt that when he and his followers were forced out of St. George Methodist Episcopal Church, God was with them.[16] This feeling of "God with us" not only kept Allen encouraged, but it gave him a kind of inexhaustible hope. God represented the highest expression of justice, righteousness, goodness, dignity, holiness, and power. Therefore, Allen felt that as long as his actions were in accordance with God's justice, righteousness, et cetera, then he did not have to worry about man. This conception of God was a very practical, functional device in stimulating Allen toward social reform. God's being, the highest authority, gave Allen the capacity to appeal to a power beyond that of the white power-structure.

He encountered strong opposition from the Methodist Conference in his attempt to start the A.M.E. Church. Allen and his followers only wanted an independent church of their own rather than a withdrawal from the Methodist Conference. However, in an attempt to stop the

31

creation of the independent A.M.E. Church, the Methodist Conference threatened to publicly turn them out of the Conference and disown them. John McClaskey called upon them as a representative of the Conference and insisted that they stop organizing their church and submit to the Conference. In response, Allen and his followers insisted upon maintaining their independence but expressed a willingness to abide by the discipline of the Methodist Church. However, in spite of this, the Methodists finally turned Allen and his followers out of the Conference. Allen maintained a firm stand with God and a determination to build an independent church for blacks. He firmly believed that God was with him in this situation; therefore, he did not fear being turned out and disowned by the Methodist Conference. He did not fear man as an authority figure, because his ultimate allegiance was to God who transcended all forms of power and authority. In describing this situation Allen said, "We bore much persecution from many of the Methodist connection; but we have reason to be thankful to Almighty God, who was our deliverer." [17]

After Allen and his followers succeeded in erecting an independent black church, in spite of extreme opposition from the Methodist Conference, they were told that if they would not turn their church over to the Methodist Conference, they could not wear the name *Methodist*. Allen responded, "We told [them they] might deny us their name, but they could not deny us a seat in Heaven." [18] Here again, Allen appealed to a greater power than the Methodist Church or man as a way of opposing injustice, racism, oppression, and man's inhumanity.

Man

Allen's theological anthropology was interwoven with his conception of God. His conception was determinative

32

in the way he understood man. The first task he had to accomplish in his conception of man was a feeling of significance, or self-worth. In every respect, slavery taught Allen and other enslaved black Americans that they were nobody and unwanted. They were not defined as genuine, authentic persons, they were defined as property to be bought or sold. The whites considered themselves superior to the black Americans; therefore, the whites developed an "I-it" relationship with the slaves rather than an "I-thou" relationship. The only value a slave had was as a utility. When he ceased to have potential productivity, he was put aside and considered obsolete. The slaves who showed great productive potential were either auctioned off or were bred like animals. There were many incidents perpetrated by Allen's slave master, the institution of slavery itself, and racism in general to press upon Allen's mind a feeling of inferiority.

A negative experience Allen had was precipitated by his slave master Stokeley who, even after conversion, was not able to think of Allen as an authentic human being. The interesting question raised by this experience is, Why didn't Stokeley permit Allen to go free without having to purchase his freedom? One reason is that even after Stokeley was converted, Allen to him remained property or a utility. Allen was an "I-it" to Stokeley rather than an "I-thou." Despite Allen's admiration for his master, who he referred to as a good, kind, affectionate one, Allen thought of slavery as "a bitter pill." Allen was very conscious of the demoralizing, inhuman "I-it" relationship that characterized the master-slave encounter. Where, then, could Allen go for support in attempting to see himself as an authentic human being with value, purpose, meaning, and possibilities for making significant contributions to mankind?

One source of support Allen received that assisted him

in the affirmation of himself and other black Americans as authentic human beings was his encounter with God. He saw himself as somebody because God loved him enough to save him from his sins; he was a child of God. In God's eyes he was not a slave, and neither was he inferior. But, rather, he felt that he and all black Americans were important in the eyes of God. And, on the basis of this theistic affirmation of the self, Allen challenged the tendency of slave masters to think of black Americans as being inferior or less than human. He challenged the slave masters to take a few black children "and cultivate their minds with the same care and let them have the same prospect in view as to living in the world, as [they] would wish for their own children, [they] would find upon the trial, they were not inferior in mental endowments." [19]

Eschatology and Ethics

Allen's eschatology was grounded in his assessment of slavery. He developed a dual eschatological approach to the eradication of slavery; he also based this perspective on a profound trust in God. And, his trust in God greatly affected his ethics. Did he feel that slavery would be eradicated in his day, thus making his eschatology, in part, this-worldly? Or, did he feel that it would be eliminated in the next world, thus making his eschatology, in part, otherworldly? It is apparent that both eschatological views were present in Allen's theology.

First, Allen argued that God hates slavery and has destroyed "kings and princes for their oppression of the poor slaves." [20] And, since God hates slavery and has obliterated it in the past, Allen felt that it was legitimate and Christian to hate and oppose slavery. He argued that God was the first to plead the cause of slaves; Allen's reference was to the Israelites in Egypt. He contended that

RICHARD ALLEN (1760 – 1831)

God led the Israelites out of slavery with a mighty hand, and, just as he led the Israelites, he will also lead black Americans out of slavery. Because Allen believed so firmly in the omnipotence and intrinsic goodness of God, he felt that slavery would inevitably be eradicated because it was in contradiction to God's intrinsic goodness. Allen saw his role as prophet, but not as avenger. God in his own time would intervene and put an end to oppression, slavery, man's inhumanity to man, and all forms of evil. Therefore, Allen challenged the slave masters to free the slaves, because slavery was unchristian and morally wrong; it was their Christian duty to let the slaves go free.

> If you love your children, if you love your country, if you love the God of love, clear your hands from slaves; burden not your children or your country with them. My heart has been sorry for the blood shed of the oppressors, as well as the oppressed; both appear guilty of each other's blood, in the sight of him who hath said, "He that sheddeth man's blood, by man shall his blood be shed."[21]

Allen was giving the slave masters a sufficient chance to repent of their sins before God, their country, black Americans, and themselves. He appealed to their good-will, their moral conscience, their sense of right and wrong, and their sense of Christian duty and responsibility. Allen's call for ethical decision-making was a call of urgency. The call was for the slave masters to repent and free the slaves. He felt that if they should take heed to the voice of God and repent, they could avoid any possible vengeance or resulting damnation. But what would happen if the slave masters did not repent?

Although Allen himself did not call for violent rebellion as a means of eradicating slavery, he saw it as being not only an inevitable consequence of the slave masters' refusal to free the slaves voluntarily but as an instrument of God as the last resort. Since Allen felt that God was the one with the power and capacity to eradicate slavery, he felt that God used both moral suasion and violent force to accomplish his goal; and, being a firm believer in the goodness, justice, power, and righteousness of God, Allen did not question the ways of God. Whatever means God saw fit to accomplish his goal were acceptable to Allen. Being grounded in Old Testament history, Allen believed that if the oppressor would not respond to moral suasion, God would then use force in accomplishing his goal. So it was, as Allen reminded the slave masters, with Pharaoh and his princes. When Pharaoh did not respond to moral suasion, God then led his people out of slavery by force. Allen argued that God chooses certain people to perform his good. The shedding of any person's blood is bad, and Allen tried to avoid this by appealing to the moral conscience of both the oppressed and the oppressors. But, Allen said that if God's word is not heard, then he uses force to accomplish his goal. The slave insurrections, according to Allen, were God's instrument for accomplishing his goal. Since the slave masters would not obey God, they left him with no choice.

> The dreadful insurrections they have made when opportunity has offered, is enough to convince a reasonable man that great uneasiness and not contentment is the inhabitant of their hearts. God himself hath pleaded their cause; He hath from time to time raised up instruments for that purpose, sometimes mean and contemptible in your sight, at other times he hath used such as it hath pleased him, with whom you have not thought it beneath your dignitiy to contend. [22]

Allen, in his quest for the freedom of black Americans, did not do it on the basis of hatred for the white slave masters. However, this is not to say that Allen took a moderate stand on the problem of slavery. But, what it means is that Allen attempted to humanize the inhumanity exemplified by the slave masters themselves. In other words, he did not meet hate with hate or inhumanity with inhumanity. Allen hated the institution of slavery; he hated the evil acts the slave masters used to perpetuate the oppression and slavery of black Americans. He hated the deeds but not the persons committing the deeds. His call to them to repent of their sins and free the slaves is a case in point of his concern for liberating both the oppressed and the oppressors, as well as being an expression of his love for America. He knew that if slavery were not voluntarily eradicated by the slave masters, it would be eradicated by God in a way that might destroy both the oppressors and the oppressed. At this point it appears that Allen anticipated the Civil War which almost destroyed America and the slaveholders as well.

Allen encouraged the slaves to love their slave masters rather than hate them. He felt that the nature of being a Christian meant for one to love his enemies and do good to those who hate and despitefully use him.[23] Therefore, in spite of the hypocrisy, racism, non-Christian attitudes, and inhuman acts of the slaveholders, Allen insisted on a superior Christian and human quality of life from the slaves. He attempted to introduce into the mainstream of America the true meaning of Christianity, love, brother-hood, justice, righteousness, and humanization. This attitude was very significant because the usual tendency of one who is oppressed and hated by another is to oppress the oppressor and to hate in return.

Unfortunately, we have distorted the true meaning of love as understood historically by black theologians. It is evident that when Allen instructed the slaves to love their enemies he did not mean for them to accept their

37

oppressive condition and to become passive. He did not mean that they should not attempt to do anything about their condition. But rather he meant that in the process of eradicating slavery and oppression, one is not to hate the oppressor but to hate the evilness of oppression. Allen saw this as being consistent with the meaning of love that comes from the Old Testament.

> That God, who knows the hearts of all men, and the propensity of a slave to hate his oppressor, hath strickly forbidden it to his chosen people, "Thou shalt not abhor an Egyptian, because thou was a stranger in his land." Deut. 23,7. [24]

True love is not always passive, accommodative, and nonresistant; but true love at its core contains a dialectic. At points it assumes a militant, aggressive, resistant role, and at other points it assumes the opposite. Therefore, knowing this dialectical meaning of love, Allen challenged the slaves to love the slaveholders as their Christian duty—never to accept slavery and oppression, never to condone it, to resist it and try to get the slaveholders to repent of the sin of slavery before God destroyed them.

Contribution

In looking at Richard Allen's contribution to the history of religion in America, one should begin with his conversion experience. The question could be raised, Why begin there? In the first place, one should begin there because it served as the foundation of Allen's entire ministry. Second, it shows a point at which Allen synthesized spiritualization and social transformation. When he converted he felt an internal freedom and liberation that led to his quest for physical freedom and liberation. He did not dichotomize spiritual liberation and physical liberation, rather he sought to liberate the whole man.

His protest of the segregated, discriminatory, and racist conditions that St. George Methodist Episcopal Church attempted to impose upon him shows that he perceived an interrelation between physical liberation and spiritual liberation. In other words, Allen did not believe that one could serve God honestly in bondage, affliction, and oppression. He walked out of St. George Church in protest of these conditions.

The origination and establishment of the A.M.E. Church under the leadership of Richard Allen contributed significantly toward the development of independence, self-determination, self-development, and self-respect within the black community. In this regard, Allen pioneered in developing black nationalism and black theology. For both black nationalism and black theology attempt to implant a value system within the black community. Within St. George Church, blacks were not free to worship and express themselves to God as they pleased; they were dependent totally on the church. But when the A.M.E. Church was created under the guidance of Richard Allen, black Americans began to realize the significance and value of having their own religious institutions. When black Americans realized that they had the ability and capacity to develop their own religious institutions, they then began to develop educational and social institutions as well as political organizations. The A.M.E. Church was officially organized in 1816 in Philadelphia, with Richard Allen as the first bishop; the first annual Negro Convention met in 1830 in Philadelphia with Richard Allen as president. The black church became the vanguard of social activism.

Allen's theological suppositions served as the foundation of his social activism. He used his conceptions of God, man, eschatology, and ethics to protest slavery, racism, segregation, oppression and to humanize the inhumanity existing in America.

Chapter III
David Walker
1785–1830

Early Life and Development

David Walker was born to a free black woman and an enslaved black man in Wilmington, North Carolina. Walker, therefore, was born free because the law in the slave states stipulated that the status of the children would be the same as the mother's, not the father's. It is believed that Walker's father died before David's birth, but his mother gave to Walker not only freedom but a resentment of the institution of slavery as well.[1] His burning indignation toward the institution of slavery became so acute that he could not tolerate living in the South.

> If I remain in this bloody land, I will not live long. As true as God reigns, I will be avenged for the sorrow which my people have suffered. This is not the place for me—no, no. I must leave this part of the country. It will be a great trial for me to live on the same soil where so many men are in slavery; certainly I cannot remain where I must hear their chains continually and where I must encounter the insults of their hypocritical enslavers.[2]

From the above statement it is apparent that Walker had a profound love for his people. Being a free man, he could have attempted to set himself apart from his enslaved brethren, but he realized that his own freedom was inextricably bound up with the freedom of the enslaved.

41

In other words, he could not be free in the true sense of the word until the institution of slavery was abolished. Therefore, his love for humanity forced him to detest and repudiate the conditions of oppression that dehumanized and enslaved his brethren. Thus, rather than remain in the South where these oppressive, inhuman conditions were continually being perpetrated upon black Americans, Walker decided to leave the South. After leaving, Walker settled in Boston, Massachusetts, where he was educated. In 1827 he became the proprietor of a clothing business on Brattle Street.

The question may be asked, How did Walker make such an acute assessment of the oppressive, inhuman conditions of slavery since he was not a slave? His own testimony was that he traveled over a considerable portion of the United States, including both the South and the North. In the course of his travels he made very accurate observations of the conditions of slavery. As a result of these observations, Walker came to the conclusion that black Americans were "the most degraded, wretched, and abject set of beings that ever lived since the world began." [3] He felt that slavery in the United States could not be compared to any form of slavery historically or contemporaneously. He argued that American slavery was the worst form of slavery. He said that the slavery that existed among the Israelites in Egypt, the Greeks in Greece, the Romans in Rome, and other people in other places was not as severe, cruel, degrading, and dehumanizing as that in America.

He was particularly critical of American slavery, because America professed to be a Christian nation. He felt that this was the worst kind of hypocrisy. In fact, throughout the *Appeal*, Walker is critical of the hypocrisy of America in its theory and practice. In other words, America professed to be Christian, but in actuality its practice, in terms of the institution of slavery, was in total opposition to the principles that Christianity is based on. But in spite of the evils of slavery and oppression, Walker maintained an abiding hope for the ultimate redemption of America. He insisted that black Americans should continue the fight for freedom and justice rather than become frustrated, pessimistic, and look toward Africa for ultimate redemption and liberation. At this point in his career, David Walker was very much influenced by the life and thought of Richard Allen.

Richard Allen and David Walker on the American Colonization Society

David Walker was greatly impressed with the courage and perseverance Allen exemplified in the origination and development of the African Methodist Episcopal Church. He felt that this church was as durable as any church could possibly be. Because of his many outstanding contributions, Walker anticipated the time when Richard Allen could emerge as a landmark in the history of religion in America.

Why did Walker believe in the ultimate redemption of America, and how did the thoughts of Richard Allen contribute to it? Allen was bitterly opposed to the colonizing of Africans in Liberia. In 1822 Liberia, on the West Coast of Africa, was designated by the American Colonization Society as the place to deport black Americans from America. In large measure, the American Colonization Society geared itself toward the deportation of free blacks. The Society received strong support from the U.S. Congress, bequests, gifts, church groups, state legislatures, and auxiliary societies. The rationale of the Society was to deport free blacks to Africa so that they could "Christianize" the "heathens." Some blacks accepted this idea and returned to Africa, but the majority of blacks bitterly rejected it. Richard Allen and David Walker were two prominent, articulate spokesmen in opposition to the ideas, principles, goals, and direction of the American Colonization Society.

They opposed it on the grounds that America was the black man's home. This, of course, was not negating Africa or rejecting it as the birthplace and original homeland of black Americans. But Allen and Walker felt that black Americans had built America with their own hands. Many had fought in the American Revolution to protect the freedom of America, and many had given their lives for America. Therefore, Allen and Walker believed that for blacks to return to Africa would make things too convenient for America. They sought, then, to challenge America to repudiate itself from the evils of slavery and oppression and to live out the full meaning of the Christian principles on which the country was built.

Theology of David Walker

God and Black Suffering

In his conception of God, Walker found himself faced with the major problem in theodicy. The term *theodicy* comes from two Greek words meaning "deity" and "justice"; it concerns itself with the attempt to justify the goodness of God in face of the manifold presence of evil in the world. The major problem in theodicy is the attempt to resolve this paradoxical dilemma: If God is all-powerful and all-merciful, why doesn't he eliminate evil in the world? If he is not able to eliminate evil in the world, then he is not all-powerful. If he is able to eliminate evil in the world and chooses not to, then he is not all-merciful. In spite of this paradoxical dilemma, theists have traditionally exonerated God and have not held him responsible for the presence of evil and suffering in the world.

Walker found himself defending the goodness and justice of God in the face of the presence of black suffering. He did not try to resolve the paradoxical dilemma in theodicy, however, but he affirmed the goodness and justice of God in spite of the paradoxical dilemma. He felt that God was all-powerful, righteous, just, merciful, revengeful, and sovereign.

He developed his conception of God in protest to the institution of slavery. God, for Walker, was not the result of some systematic philosophical-theological formulation, but rather God, for Walker, developed out of the context of black oppression. Therefore, Walker's conception of God is grounded in the social, economic, political, and educational foundations of America. There is obviously no dichotomy between the spiritual and the physical in Walker's conception of God. He sees the spiritual and the physical as organic, interdependent realities. He felt that God was as concerned with the black man's physical liberation as he was with his spiritual liberation.

Why did Walker think of God as all-powerful? In the first place Walker himself along with all the other black Americans of his day was powerless politically, educationally, and economically. The slaveholders tried to project themselves over the slaves as masters to be worshiped, honored, and respected. The slaveholders believed that they were predestined to be masters and that blacks were predestined to be slaves. The slaveholders believed that they represented the greatest source of power to the slaves because they controlled the social, educational, economic, and political institutions. The slaveholders, therefore, demanded that the slaves refer to them as "master." In protest to this, Walker said, "They forget that God rules in the armies of heaven and among the inhabitants of the earth, having his ears continually open to the cries, tears and groans of his oppressed people." Walker continued to challenge the slaves by raising the questions: Do we have any master but Jesus Christ? If God or Jesus Christ alone is our master, "what right then, have we to obey and call any other master but Himself?"[4]

Walker said to the slaves that they were not to look up to the slaveholders and call them master, because the same God made them all. God didn't create the master-slave relationship, but it resulted from the evils of white racism and the capitalist system which was built on cheap labor. Walker challenges the slaves to place their loyalties and allegiance in God the master, rather than in the slaveholders. He goes further to challenge the slaves to obey God rather than the slaveholders. It follows then, as Walker viewed it, that anyone who supported or condoned slavery was in opposition to God because slavery was against the will of God. And anyone who attempted to eradicate slavery was in conformity with the will of God. Walker argued that God did not create anyone to be a slave. God created all men free, and thus when anyone violates this freedom it becomes the responsibility of the oppressed to eradicate the oppression. But since the slaves were powerless, how were they to disarm the slaveholders?

Walker argued that God, through his omnipotence, would one day appear in behalf of the oppressed and eradicate the oppression of slaves. Walker challenged the slaves that it was their moral responsibility to participate with God in the abolition of slavery. Although Walker felt that God was quite capable of eliminating slavery and

46

oppression, he did not minimize the black man's role in this process. It was his contention that black Americans were morally obligated to maximize their efforts toward the achievement of freedom, and God would assure them of this freedom. He based this assurance of freedom on the justice of God. The justice of God was in total opposition to slavery and oppression. This made the condition of slavery and the justice of God a paradox in the mind of Walker.

Walker did not attempt to resolve this paradox by renouncing his faith in God or by making God responsible for the oppression of black Americans. But because of his firm belief in justice and the omnipotence of God, Walker argued that because of God the freedom of black Americans was inevitable. He raises the questions:

> Is not God a God of justice to all his creatures? Do you say he is? Then if he gives peace and tranquility to tyrants, and permits them to keep our fathers, our mothers, ourselves and our children in eternal ignorance and wretchedness, to support them and their families, would he be to us a God of justice?[5]

The above questions raised by Walker repudiated the belief held by many slaveholders that black Americans were predestined by God to be slaves. The slaveholders used every means available, including the Bible, to convince the slaves that they were predestined by God and were eternally fixed to be slaves. Walker, of course, reversed this process and argued that black Americans were predestined by God to be free. The slaveholders used biblical passages to indoctrinate the slaves into believing that God had called them to be slaves. An example of such biblical passages is:

> Let every soul be subject unto the higher powers. For there is no power but of God: the powers that be are ordained of

47

God. Whosoever therefore resisteth the power, resisted the ordinance of God: and they that resist shall receive to themselves damnation. (Rom. 13:1-2)

Walker challenged the slaves to fear not the number and education of the slaveholders against whom they had to contend for their freedom, which was guaranteed to them by God. He asked, Why should we be afraid when God is now and will continue to be on our side? With this profound faith in God, Walker said to the slaves, If you will not fight with God in the glorious and heavenly cause of freedom to be delivered from the most wretched form of slavery since the foundation of the world then, you ought to be kept in slavery.[6]

Eschatology and Redemption

When did Walker feel that the slavery and oppression of black Americans would be eliminated? Did he think of this in otherworldly eschatological terms or in this-worldly eschatological terms? One of the distorted images of black religion that we have gleaned from historians, sociologists, religionists, and theologians is that it is fundamentally otherworldly and escape-oriented. Walker's eschatology clearly shows that the heart of black religion is protest- and liberation-oriented. Walker did not pacify the slaves with an escape-oriented, otherworldly eschatology; he insisted that God would bring the sufferings and oppression of blacks to an end in spite of the slaveholders' attempt to perpetuate the institution of slavery. He argued that God was going to do this on this side of eternity, in this life.[7]

Walker contended that God would send a deliverer to lead the slaves to freedom and victory. He was very doubtful as to whether the slaveholders would free the slaves without physical force or violence. If America, he

48

said to the slaves, in its refusal to free the slaves, forces God to use physical force to accomplish his will, then give the deliverer that God gives you, your fullest support. By giving him support, Walker felt that the slaves would not only enhance their freedom and liberation but would behold in him the salvation of God. "God will indeed, deliver you through him from your deplorable and wretched condition under the Christians of America. I charge you this day before my God to lay no obstacle in his way, but let him go." [8]

Repentance

It was not Walker's desire that the slaveholders be destroyed, but rather that the institution of slavery be destroyed. It was his firm belief that the slaveholders and all those who supported the institution of slavery would adhere to the voice of God and repent of their sins. He felt that God was giving America a chance to repent and free the slaves. He said, "I would like to see the whites repent peradventure God may have mercy on them." Walker argued that unless America repented and freed the slaves, God would disrupt America and free the slaves through physical force. "But oh Americans! Americans! I warn you in the name of the Lord (Whether you will hear, or forbear), to repent and reform or you are ruined." [9]

Not only did Walker feel that God would disrupt America unless the slaves were freed, but also that God would destroy many whites. He based his conviction on the way in which God dealt with slaveholders in the past. Walker used an example from the Bible:

I will not speak here of the destructions which the Lord brought upon Egypt, in consequence of the oppression and consequent groans of the oppressed—of the hundreds and thousands of Egyptians whom God hurled into the Red Sea for afflicting his people in their land. [10]

49

Walker's call to repentance was a call of urgency. He challenged America to make a decision about slavery without any procrastination. He was convinced that slavery could not continue because God in his justice would not tolerate it. Thus, God would destroy any forces that attempted to support and perpetuate the institution of slavery.

Contribution

One cannot overly emphasize the significance of David Walker. His struggles represent one of the earliest attempts to systematically speak to the problem of the paradox between an all-powerful and all-loving God and the presence of evil and black suffering in the world. Walker, of course, attempted to resolve this paradox by exonerating God in spite of the manifold presence of evil in the world. The idea he propounded was that, ultimately, black suffering would be inevitably eliminated because it was in opposition to the will, purpose, and divine plan of God. He saw God as the liberator who assured black Americans of ultimate victory over slavery, oppression, and suffering. Along with Richard Allen, Walker believed that if the slaveholders and America did not repent and free the slaves, then God in his omnipotence would rise up and use force to eliminate the institution of slavery. It is apparent that both Allen and Walker anticipated the Civil War. But it is important to note that the prophetic words of Allen's and Walker's represented attempts to avoid the Civil War by trying to get America to eradicate slavery voluntarily.

Walker developed a dual eschatological hope orientation. It contained both vertical and horizontal dimensions, that is, his hope for the future called for freedom both within and beyond history. He did not believe that black Americans should wait patiently for God to satisfy their thirst for freedom and justice in heaven. His theological thrust was not passive, docile, submissive, or obedient to the slaveholders. He challenged the slaves to seek freedom and liberation in this world, to resist slavery, and never to accept or submit to slavery and oppression. This represented a kind of this-worldly eschatological hope. But Walker was careful not to repudiate other-worldly eschatology. This played a significant role in Walker's theology.

Chapter IV
Nat Turner
1800?–1831

Early Life and Development

Nat Turner was born in Southampton County, Virginia, around October 2, 1800, the property of Benjamin Turner. He was an unusual child and felt called very early to be a prophet. His parents were very inspirational and supportive of his claim to have been called by God for some special purpose. He said that his parents strengthened his claim of faith by saying in his presence that he was intended for some great purpose because of certain marks on his head and breast. Not only did Turner's parents support his faith claim of being called for some special purpose, but his peers supported it as well. In fact, many of the slaves within the immediate Southampton community were supportive of Turner's claim. And, this support significantly contributed to the continued spiritual development of Nat Turner.

All the external forces that Nat Turner and the other slaves were surrounded with were attempting to indoctrinate Nat Turner into believing that he was a nobody. Blacks at this time were not defined as human beings; they were defined as property to be bought and sold. Therefore, the very nature of slavery, as Nat Turner experienced it, was a force that degraded the individual. But in the midst of the external dehumanizing forces of slavery, Nat Turner was able to say first, I am somebody because I am a child of God, and second, I am going to make a great contribution to mankind. At this early stage, Nat Turner did not fully understand the kind of contribution that he was going to make, but he believed that it was going to be something significant.

Turner's aspiration to make a contribution to humanity was based on his precociousness. He realized that he was an unusual child with exceptional ability. He was very observant and inquisitive of everything; he was attentive to everything that he saw and heard. He said that he even fascinated himself because of his unusual capacity to learn to read. He learned to read with perfect ease and astonished both himself and the black community of Southampton County. Whenever he got the chance to read books, he found in them many things that he himself had reflected upon in his moments of imagination, contemplation, and reflection. This reinforced in him his own sense of having exceptional ability.

Theology of Nat Turner
Messianic Call

It is apparent in Turner's confessions that the special purpose that he felt called for was of a messianic nature, messianic in the sense that he felt called by God to lead his people out of the bondage of slavery and oppression. The idea of a messiah's being sent by God to lead the slaves out of bondage was very popular during the antebellum period. This messianic concept was connected with the belief that God was going to eliminate slavery by his omnipotent power and that he was going to raise up a messiah to lead the people. David Walker's *Appeal* contains this idea:

> Beloved brethren—here let me tell you, and believe it, that the Lord our God, as true as he sits on his throne in heaven,

and as true as our Savior died to redeem the world, will give you a Hannibal; the person whom God shall give you, give your support and let him go his death, and behold in him the salvation of your God. God will indeed, deliver you through him from your deplorable and wretched condition under the Christians of America. I charge you this day before my God to lay no obstacle in his way, but let him go.[1]

It is believed that Nat Turner got a copy of the Walker *Appeal* when it was being circulated in Virginia, and having read the above section he saw himself as the fulfillment of Walker's prophecy that God was going to send a messiah to liberate the slaves from oppression and bondage.[2] Believing that he was the messiah, Nat Turner gave himself to constant fasting and prayer in preparation for the great task of liberating the slaves. Turner realized that the task of liberating the slaves from bondage was a very difficult one and that it required maximum preparation spiritually and strategically. Therefore, at every point he attempted to follow God rather than his intuition and insights. It is evident that he made every attempt to be as careful and sure about his actions as possible. As long as he felt that his actions were in conformity with God's will, he was not troubled.

Nat Turner was very much impressed by the particular passage of scripture that says, "Seek ye first the kingdom of God, . . . and all these things shall be added unto you" (Matt. 6:33). He said that he reflected a great deal on this passage and prayed daily for its understanding. Based on his understanding of this scripture, Nat Turner committed himself to pleasing and obeying God rather than man and perceived his prophetic role as being in harmony with the prophets in the Bible. He believed that the same spirit of God that spoke to the prophets of old was speaking to him. This revelatory experience further confirmed Nat's belief that he was ordained by God for some great purpose. He felt that the fulfillment of this great purpose was imminent, but he did not know just how it was going to develop. He shared these revelatory insights with his peers, and they were astonished and believed that the wisdom of Nat Turner was of divine origin. He shared his revelatory insights with his peers because he wanted to prepare them for the imminent fulfillment of his mission.[3]

Liberation Theology

Nat Turner was not a theoretician, because he did not develop a theological system, and he did not reflect on the nature and meaning of theology; Walker's *Appeal* performed this task for him. Walker's *Appeal*, as we have observed, constituted the theoretical foundation for the Nat Turner revolt. It gave the rationale and justification for revolutionary activity, and Nat Turner put the theory into practice. Nat Turner was, as Lerone Bennett, Jr., said, "David Walker's word made flesh."[4] Therefore, Nat Turner's liberation theology should be interpreted as a theology of action.

Nat's commitment to the liberation of the slaves from bondage was tested when he ran away for thirty days. His peers thought that Nat had made his escape as his father had done, but to their amazement Turner returned. It is true that Nat could have escaped within the thirty-day period, but his return indicated a definite commitment to the cause of liberation. He was more interested in freeing his brothers and sisters from bondage and oppression than he was in saving himself. Upon returning he had a vision that had an overwhelming effect upon his life.

In this vision Nat saw white spirits and black spirits engaged in battle. He then saw the sun darken, heard thunder rolling in the heavens, saw blood flowing in streams, and heard a voice saying, "Such is your luck, such you are called to see, and let it come rough or smooth, you must surely bear it."[5] This vision said to Nat that his effort was to be put toward the liberation of the slaves through bloodshed and violence. Nat himself was not a violent man, but the situation of slavery, oppression, and racism forced violence upon him. He knew that violence was the only thing that would force America to take the slaves' quest for freedom and justice seriously; not only did Nat realize this, but God realized it as well. God spake through David Walker in 1829 and warned America that violence and bloodshed would result if the slaves were not freed. But rather than adhere to the voice of God as uttered through David Walker in the *Appeal*, the slaveholding states tried to suppress, destroy, and censure Walker's *Appeal*, thus making the Nat Turner revolt inevitable. Did Nat Turner attempt other methods of liberation, or was he just a bloodthirsty, angry black revolutionary?

There were essentially three approaches used by the abolitionist for liberation.[6] There were moral suasion, political action, and physical resistance. Nat Turner was not an exponent of moral suasion nor political action. He felt led by God to liberate the slaves with physical resistance only. David Walker advocated moral suasion in the *Appeal* when he called upon America to repent and free the slaves. Walker appealed to the moral conscious of America in hopes of avoiding a revolt such as Nat Turner's. And since Walker's *Appeal* did not persuade the slaveholders to free the slaves, Nat Turner chose not to write another appeal of moral suasion but rather to put the already existing one into action. But, the Nat Turner revolt could have been avoided if America would have only listened very seriously to David Walker when he said, "O Americans! I call God— I call angels— I call man, to witness, that your destruction is at hand, and will be speedily consummated unless you repent."[7] And, since

America increased the yoke of slavery rather than repent, Nat Turner perceived his role as one of physical liberation.

After seeing this vision in 1825 and after observing many miracles wrought by God to confirm to Nat that the vision was divinely inspired, Nat said that the Holy Ghost revealed to him the meaning of the vision. One of the miracles that Nat observed was "drops of blood on the corn as though it were dew from heaven." He interpreted this to mean that as the blood of Christ was shed for sinners, it was returning again and that Christ was about to lay down the yoke he had borne for the sins of man, and the great day of judgment was at hand. [8] Nat knew that the shedding of blood was a prerequisite for redemption; he had a sufficient knowledge of the Bible to realize this truth. He also knew that it was going to take the shedding of the blood of both blacks and whites before the slaves would be free; he felt that the visions and the miracles confirmed this truth.

On May 12, 1828, Nat Turner heard a loud noise in the heavens, and the Spirit said unto him, The serpent is loosened, and Christ has laid down the yoke he has borne for the sins of men, and you should take it on and fight against the serpent. [9] After this revelatory experience, Nat Turner was convinced beyond the shadow of a doubt that the bloody battle that he was to begin was very near. When Nat accepted his call to liberate the slaves, he knew that his ultimate fate would be death, but this revelatory experience encouraged him by reminding him that Christ died for the sins of the world. Nat then felt prepared to give his life for the cause of freedom and liberation. He firmly believed that both his effort and final death would be redemptive in bringing slavery to an end.

Every step that Nat Turner took in preparation for the revolt was, according to his own words, under the direction and guidance of God. He refused to begin the revolt without a sign from God. On the appearance of a sign from heaven, Nat felt that he should arise and prepare himself to slay his enemies with their own weapons.[10] This sign appeared in February, 1831, and consisted of an eclipse of the sun. He recruited four trusted friends, Hark, Henry, Nelson, and Sam, to participate in the revolt with him. Their plan was to strike on July 4, but Nat became ill and delayed the revolt. Another sign appeared to Nat that was in the form of a peculiar color of the sun. Nat then set August 13, 1831, as the day for the revolt. At the proper time Nat and his four friends began the revolt that shook the foundations of slavery.

Contribution

The Nat Turner revolt raises complex theological questions: What does it have to say about the problem of the ethics of violence? Was he ethically right in what he did? Is violence ever legitimate before God? Who sets the limits, man or God? For Nat's perspective God sets the limits; he determines what man must do to be saved.

The tragedy of violence that surrounded the Nat Turner revolt did not lie in the killings that Nat and his followers executed, but, rather, it lay in the violence of slavery. The institution of slavery itself contained all sorts of violence. There was psychological violence which did great damage to the slaves; many were brainwashed into believing that they were predestined by God to be slaves. Everything about the institution of slavery said to the slaves that they were nobody, less than human. It was this kind of psychological violence that significantly contributed to the Nat Turner revolt. When looked at in this way, the Nat Turner revolt was a response to violence. Not only was there psychological violence perpetrated upon the slaves, but economic exploitation, social degradation, and physical violence as well. The following questions can be asked: Does the end justify the means? Should one use violence to fight violence? Does the Christian faith stand in opposition to violence regardless of the situation? How is one to understand the ethics of violence in light of the Christian faith?

When looked at theologically, the problem of violence in light of the Nat Turner revolt becomes a question of survival. The institution of slavery was so severe and rigid that it gave Turner no alternative other than violence. Moral suasion was used as a liberation strategy by Richard Allen, David Walker, and others, but it failed to convince the slaveholders that slavery was sinful in the sight of God and therefore should be abolished. Slavery had become so embedded into the matrix of America until the slaveholding states were insensitive to the moans and groans of the slaves. Both Richard Allen and David Walker anticipated the Nat Turner revolt and the Civil War. For when Richard Allen and David Walker challenged the institution of slavery, they both called upon the slaveholders to repent and free the slaves. But, because in the eyes of the slaveholders Richard Allen and David Walker did not represent power, they did not pose a threat to slavery itself. But both prophets said to the slaveholders and to America that if you do not repent of your sins and free the slaves, God will send violence upon you. Upon the continued refusal of the slaveholders to free the slaves, Richard Allen argued that God would use dreadful insurrections as instruments to free the slaves. He reminded the slaveholders how God in his omnipotence destroyed kings and princes for their oppression of the slaves; he mentioned that Pharaoh and his army were destroyed by God. Thus, since the slaves were powerless,

Allen contended that God became their avenger.[11] David Walker picked up this same theme and said to the slaveholders, "Your DESTRUCTION is at hand, and will be speedily consummated unless you repent."[12] It is clear here that both Richard Allen and David Walker used moral suasion in the attempt to prick the moral conscience of the slaveholders so that they would feel guilty and shameful about the moral evils of slavery. But rather than repent and abolish slavery, the slaveholders made slavery more severe and inhuman, thus encouraging the physical violence of Nat Turner.

This raises a serious question about the possibility and power of moral suasion as a strategy used for eliminating slavery, oppression, and man's inhumanity to man. Not only did the slaveholders refuse to take seriously the prophetic utterances of Richard Allen's and David Walker's, but even after the Nat Turner revolt they refused to free the slaves; this refusal significantly contributed to the start of the Civil War.

Chapter V
Daniel Alexander Payne
1811–1893

Significant Events
in the Early Life of Payne

Daniel Alexander Payne was born on February 24, 1811, to free parents in Charleston, South Carolina. Both of his parents died while he was very young, and he began working when he was twelve years old.

Very early he developed a great fascination for books, education, and the discovery of new things. During the time that he was working in a carpenter's shop, he became exposed to the "Self Interpreting Bible." The preface to this Bible contained a brief biographical sketch of John Brown of Haddington, Scotland. It revealed that Brown mastered Latin, Greek, and Hebrew without a teacher. Payne then asked, If Brown learned Latin, Greek, and Hebrew without a living teacher, why can't I?[1] Payne decided that he would try it. Up to this time, Payne had never seen a Latin, Greek, or Hebrew volume, but his aspiration was to get one and study it.

He became a convert when he was eighteen years old. Several weeks after his conversion experience he had a unique encounter with God that he considered determinative in his life. He heard the spirit of God saying to him, "I have set thee apart to educate thyself in order that thou mayest be an educator to thy people."[2] After this encounter with God, Payne decided to commit himself to the ministry of education. He devoted every moment of leisure to the study and purchase of books. He soon forsook the carpenter's trade and decided to become an educator.

Since Payne felt commissioned by God to be an educator, he was willing to sacrifice everything for the cause of education. A slaveholder offered Payne the opportunity of working in the West Indies; he felt that this opportunity would advance Payne both educationally and economically. He even went to the extent of telling Payne that the thing that made the difference between the slave master and the slave was superior knowledge. Upon hearing this statement, Payne immediately declined the slaveholder's offer to accompany him to the West Indies and replied, "If it is true that there is nothing but superior knowledge between the master and the slave . . . I will go and obtain that knowledge which constitutes the master."[3]

Payne's first school was opened in 1829; it consisted of three children from whom he received fifty cents each a month. For the same price he taught three adults at night which made his total income three dollars per month.[4] This remuneration was insufficient for Payne to survive on, and because of it he considered closing his school and desired to find other employment. However, after his negative experience with the slaveholder, concerning the work trip to the West Indies and superior education's being the distinguishing factor between the slave and the master, Payne decided to reopen his school in spite of his economic crisis. His school, then, began to grow very rapidly, and he assessed it as a great success. But this only lasted for a short time.

62

DANIEL ALEXANDER PAYNE (1811 – 1893)

In 1834 the General Assembly of South Carolina drew up a bill forbidding slaves to be taught to read and write. This bill was discussed thoroughly, was passed, and became a law to be enforced on April 1, 1835. The law said in essence that if a white person taught a slave to read or write he would be fined one hundred dollars and be imprisoned for six months. If a free black person taught a slave to read or write he would be whipped fifty lashes and fined fifty dollars. And, if one slave taught another slave to read or write he would be whipped fifty lashes.[5] After the passing of the law, Payne became very frustrated and disappointed. But in spite of it, he was determined to pursue a career as an educator, to further his education, and to continue to assist others in learning. Because of Payne's efforts in education and the efforts of other black Americans of Charleston, South Carolina, "the Negroes of Charleston were early in the nineteenth century ranked by some as economically and intellectually superior to any other such persons in the United States."[6] However, in spite of Payne's commitment and strong determination to continue the pursuit of education and to assist others in this regard, and after reflecting on the great difficulties involved in blacks' acquiring education, he began to raise some serious questions about the justice of God and the problem of evil.

Theology of Daniel Payne

God, Providence, and Evil

Because of the passing of the law forbidding slaves to learn to read and write, Payne began to wonder whose side God was on—the slaves or the slaveholders. In the midst of frustrations and difficulties, Payne said that

63

sometimes it seemed as though some wild beast had plunged its fangs into his heart and was squeezing out its life blood. He then began to question the existence of God and to say, If God does exist, then is he just? And, if God is just, why does he permit the oppressors to enslave black Americans and to rob them by unrighteous enactments of rights which they hold dear and most sacred?[7] As was true with Nathaniel Paul and David Walker, Payne raised the problem of evil. Why do righteous people suffer? Why do they meet with tragedy and misfortune? How can we reconcile the paradox between God's intrinsic goodness, his omnipotence, and black suffering?

How did Payne attempt to resolve these questions? Obviously, he didn't attempt to resolve them by repudiating and rejecting God completely; although at this point his feelings about God were very pessimistic. Basic to Payne's conception of God was the notion of divine omnipotence and sovereignty. And, in addition, he believed that God was infinite in wisdom and inexhaustible in goodness,[8] thus making the closing down of his school inconsistent with God's power and goodness. Payne could not understand why God permitted this evil to fall upon his school and his students. This event not only forced Payne to question God but also forced him to wonder about the administration of God's providence.[9] Since he believed that God reigns and the hearts of the rulers of the earth are in his hands as wax is in the hands of the artificer, he felt that God should govern history in the interest of justice and righteousness rather than the other way around.[10] Since Payne adhered to a traditional conception of divine providence, it was difficult for him to provide a satisfactory answer to the problem of evil.

In terms of his view of providence, he believed that God has a plan in history and uses force to make his plan realized. For Payne, God is infinite, holy, and righteous in all ways. He viewed God as being responsible for everything that happens in human history. If God is responsible for everything that happens in history, then how did Payne account for evil? Is God responsible for evil? Payne believed that God causes the good in history and permits the evil. But if God permits the evil, doesn't this go against God's intrinsic goodness? Or, since God permits the evil, does it mean that he is partially good? The problem in this paradox is God's sovereignty and intrinsic goodness. It became even more difficult for Payne as he reflected further on his notion of how God acts in history.

He believed that those who keep God's commandments will prosper, and those who disobey God's commandments will fall under God's wrath and indignation and will ultimately be destroyed.[11] What problem is there with Payne's reasoning at this point? If taken literally, it would appear that black Americans disobeyed God's commandments and as a result were oppressed, enslaved, and afflicted; and today these problems continue. Payne's reasoning would also suggest that the oppressors obeyed God's commandments. However, Payne himself did not mean what his reasoning seems to imply. To the contrary, he argued, "American slavery brutalizes man—destroys his moral agency, and subverts the moral government of God."[12] He believed that slavery was inconsistent with the will of God and should be abolished.

Payne hated slavery, resisted it, protested it, and called for its immediate abolishment. He argued that slavery would not allow black Americans to be Christians, because it hindered them from yielding universal and complete obedience to God, and it took away that which God granted to every man—freedom. The many things that the slaveholders forced the slaves to do, Payne felt, were in opposition to the moral law of God. For example, according to the moral law of God, adultery is forbidden. But in reference to the female slaves, Payne raised the questions: "Does the man who owns a hundred females obey the law? Does he not nullify it and compel the helpless woman to disobey God?"[13] The moral law instructed man to bring up his children under the nurture and admonition of the Lord. Payne pointed out that the slaveholders treated the slaves as property and felt that the slaves should not be brought up to serve and worship God but should serve and worship their owners. The moral law instructed children to obey their father and mother, but slavery commanded them to obey the slave master. Slavery even went to the extent of destroying the family. The moral law said, "What therefore God hath joined together, let not man put asunder" (Matt. 19:6). Payne asked, "Does not slavery nullify this law, by breaking the sacred bonds of wedlock, and separating the husband and wife forever?"[14]

Being a Christian presupposes that one studies the Scripture for spiritual renewal and illumination. Payne indicated that slavery sealed up the Word of God and made it criminal for the slave to read the Bible. Slavery never legislated for the religious instruction of slaves nor for secular instruction, but it legislated to perpetuate their ignorance.[15] Payne experienced this form of unjust legislation when his school in Charleston, South Carolina, was forced to close. God commanded those who felt called to the ministry to "go into all the world and preach the gospel to every creature." But the slave preachers were prevented from obeying this command. There were instances, though, when slave ministers were allowed to preach, but in most cases this was forbidden. And, usually when slave preachers were allowed to preach to the slaves, a white minister was required to be present. This was done to avoid any possible insurrections. But the black slave preacher was able to preach to his congregation in what E. Franklin Frazier correctly called the "invisible black church." [16] This was the plantation black church which existed in a noninstitutional fashion. It existed in spite of every attempt by the slaveholders to destroy it. It was an undercover black church. At night the slaves would slip away and meet in the woods to worship God and to organize escapes and slave insurrections. This was the black church that Nat Turner was affiliated with.

The slaves were sensitive to the oppression exercised over them by the slaveholders. They observed the slaveholders who professed to be Christian and felt that they were hypocrites because they knew that oppression and slavery were inconsistent with the Christian religion. Therefore, many of the slaves scoffed at the Christian religion, mocked their masters, and, in many instances, began to distrust both the goodness and justice of God. [17] The slaves felt that they were having their hell here on earth and the slaveholders were having their heaven. Looking at the great gulf between the social, economic, political, and intellectual conditions of the slaveholders and the slaves, and realizing the hypocrisy of the slaveholders, the slaves sang:

> But everybody talking 'bout heaven
> Ain't going there.

In spite of this, for Payne and the slaves, their dominant religious orientation was a reaffirmation of faith, an abiding belief in the reality of God and a continued hope in the future and in the promises of God.

They did not reject the Christian faith but applied it to protestation of slavery. The slave masters attempted to indoctrinate the slaves with a passive, submissive, and nonresistant view of the meaning of the Christian faith.

The genius of the slaves was that they rejected this distortion of Christianity and used it as the foundation for the abolishment of slavery. Payne reported that he observed many slaves in several instances standing at the church door while slaveholders were preaching the gospel and demanding that they go home and set their slaves free.[18]

Man

Payne bitterly resisted black inferiority and felt that blacks were of great value. He contended, following the precepts of Acts 17:26, that God made of one blood all nations of men to dwell on all the face of the earth. He, therefore, believed that in the eyes of God, blacks were accepted, significant, important, and considered persons rather than things. He had every reason to think of the slaveholders as things, because of their severe and inhuman actions against blacks. But he transcended this feeling of hatred and bitterness; he persistently hated slavery but hoped for the conversion of the slaveholders. Man, in Payne's theological interpretation, was fallen; he thought of man as a sinner. Being a sinner, Payne contended, man was capable of oppressing his neighbor. In cases of man's inhumanity to man, Payne said that the conscience, like the conviction, is blind, erroneous, misled, and perverted. [19]

Payne believed that originally man was created in the image and likeness of God, thus making man's status a little lower than the angels. But slavery, he argued, brings man down from this elevated position to the level of animals. By this Payne meant that to treat persons as property or things is not in keeping with God's purpose for man. And, in spite of the reality of slavery, the hope and encouragement that Payne had was the fact that God's love for blacks never ceased. Not only did slavery treat blacks as animals, but Payne says that it attempted to destroy the mind, will, and soul of black Americans.[20] This is why the conception of God is so important in Payne's theology and in the religious orientation of the slaves. The slave master insisted that the slaves submit their bodies, minds, wills, and souls to the perpetuation of the institution of slavery, but both Payne and the enslaved blacks contended that God is the supreme master, ruler, and governor of the universe. This meant, therefore, that man was to submit to God only, not to man. It was on this basis that Payne and other antislavery advocates opposed the institution of slavery. Man, as Payne perceived him, normally did the right thing; if his heart, conscience, and will were not in conformity with the will of God, he would do the evil thing. And, Payne viewed the evils of sin, the evils of the conscience, and the perversion of the will as being a central cause of American slavery. The source capable of establishing true liberation and reconciliation among blacks and whites was Jesus Christ. He argued that the power of God shall conquer all differences between the peoples, harmonize all conflicting views, and make us go in peace.[21] Did Payne ever see this happen?

In Washington, Pennsylvania, Payne had the opportunity of seeing a black man and a white man respond to each other in an authentic manner: they did not repudiate their ethnicity but rather accepted each other's ethnicity and judged each other not by the color of their skin but by the content of their character. Payne said that these two men had most congenial spirits, and both their actions struck him as an emphatic repudiation of the satanic lie that white men and black men are naturally antagonistic to each other.[22]

Eschatology

Payne's eschatology is interrelated with his understanding of God, history, and evil. In the first place, it is very clear that he perceived that God was in control of the historical process. He thought of God as omnipotent, sovereign, and the governor of the world. Therefore, whatever happened in history, Payne believed there was a cause for it. He had extreme difficulty, however, trying to reconcile the apparent paradox between God's sovereignty, goodness, and omnipotence, with the presence of evil and slavery. His eschatology reflects a further attempt to understand the problem of evil and God's love and power by affirming the ultimate eventuation of the good in spite of the presence of evil and slavery.

On the one hand Payne called for the immediate abolition of slavery, and on the other hand he challenged the slaves to trust in God and to trust that a better day was coming in God's eschatological future. He said, "With God one day is as a thousand years and a thousand years as one day. Trust in him, and he will bring slavery and all its outrages to an end."[23] What did Payne mean by this statement? He did not mean that the slaves were not to attempt to abolish slavery because, as we have observed, Payne called for an immediate abolition of slavery. His speech delivered before the Franckean Synod of the Evangelical Lutheran Church in support of a synodical report to end slavery in the United States is evidence that Payne wanted slavery abolished.[24]

Why was Payne opposed to slavery?

I am opposed to slavery, not because it enslaves the black man, but because it enslaves man. And were all the slaveholders in this land men of color, and the slaves white men, I would be as thorough and uncompromising an abolitionist as I now am; for whatever and whenever I may

70

see a being in the form of a man, enslaved by his fellowman, without respect to his complexion, I shall lift up my voice to plead his cause, against all the claims of his proud oppressor; and I shall do it not merely from the sympathy which man feels towards suffering man, but because God, the living God, whom I dare not disobey, has commanded me . . . to plead the cause of the oppressed.[25]

Payne made the above statement in 1839. Realizing that slavery was not going to be abolished immediately, Payne encouraged the slaves to trust in God and to trust that one day in God's sight was a thousand years in man's sight. He suggested that God had a timetable and that he would ultimately eradicate slavery according to his plan. Thus, Payne anticipated a time, eschatologically, when God would inevitably overpower the oppressors and break the yoke and chains of slavery, oppression, man's inhumanity to man, and affliction. But he felt that man had to have the patience to wait on God. Waiting on God, however, did not mean that man should not maximize his own efforts in the eradication of slavery. It meant that man had an ultimate assurance of hope and confidence that slavery was going to be abolished because God guaranteed it.

Contribution

Bishop Daniel Alexander Payne followed Nathaniel Paul, Richard Allen, David Walker, and Nat Turner in the quest for freedom and liberation. Payne's theology was, indeed, one of liberation. His conception of liberation was not as compensatory as some scholars have argued. But rather it was primarily geared toward liberation in this world. This is not to mean, however, that the eschatology of Payne was not otherworldly; it contained both this-worldly and otherworldly perspectives. Payne felt that the freedom and liberation of black Americans was inevitably coming because God had so decreed it. Payne did not exhaust his conception of liberation within a this-worldly eschatological hope but felt that there was an other-worldly hope as well. He did not believe that God was going to do all the work of liberation for black people. He contended that blacks must work with God in the quest for freedom and liberation. Slavery and oppression were opposed to God's law and, therefore, as Payne argued, must be opposed. The abolition of slavery was thus God's mandate from heaven and should be obeyed. This is why Payne felt compelled to oppose slavery, not because blacks were involved, but because of a principle. He said that he would oppose slavery regardless of the particular ethnicity of the group. Payne, like Nathaniel Paul, Richard Allen, David Walker, and Nat Turner, integrated spirituality with social reality. He did not create a dualism between the sacred and the secular but thought of liberation in light of spiritual freedom and physical freedom.

Daniel Alexander Payne pioneered in the development of religious and social movements within the nineteenth century. He not only made the black man sensitive to the need for education to function in America but also brought the black clergy to the realization of the need for an educated ministry. Because of Payne's many educational achievements, he was named official historian of his denomination, the African Methodist Episcopal Church. He joined the A.M.E. Church in 1841 and moved up to the bishopric eleven years later. Upon his appointment to the presidency of Wilberforce University, he became the first black college president in America. It is also important to note that from 1842 to 1843 Payne was a leader of the Vigilance Committee which was organized for the purpose of hiding runaway slaves from state, local, and federal authorities who sought to take the slaves back to their masters.[26] Therefore, not only should we think of Payne as an outstanding religious leader, theologian, and educator, but we should also think of him as a great abolitionist.

Chapter VI
James W. C. Pennington
1812–1871

Early Life and Development

James W. C. Pennington was a man of unusual oratory and intellectual ability. He was born a slave in 1812 on Colonel Gordon's farm in the state of Maryland. He became a blacksmith by trade and, therefore, became more valuable to his slave master. Like most slaves, Pennington was denied the opportunity to learn to read and write; however, after Pennington reached a mature age, he escaped from slavery, fled to the North, and began to educate himself. Because of his intense effort to become educated, he emerged as an unusually brilliant scholar in Greek, Latin, German, and theology. He was led into the ministry and was later ordained into the Presbyterian Church. He lived in Hartford, Connecticut, for several years and served as pastor of a church there. In later years Pennington became the pastor of the Shiloh Presbyterian Church in New York City.[1]

Because of Pennington's outstanding gift as an orator and his exceptional scholarship, he was in great demand both as a preacher and as a lecturer. He visited Europe several times in both capacities. On his third visit to Europe, "he remained there for three or four years, preaching and lecturing, during which time he atttended the Peace Congresses held at Paris, Brussels, and London."[2] While in Germany, he had the honor and distinction of having the doctor of divinity degree bestowed upon him by the University of Heidelberg.

Theology of James Pennington

The Bible and Slavery

James W. C. Pennington can be categorized as a biblical theologian; from beginning to end, his theology was grounded in the Bible. His conception of God, man, eschatology, and ethics was biblically-oriented. He felt, however, that this was not anything unique to himself, because most of the black preachers of that day were biblically-oriented in their preaching. "Our preachers are generally well versed in Biblical history."[3] One of the mysterious and unique things about black preachers, generally speaking, was that most of them knew the Bible quite thoroughly. Oral tradition played a great role; the biblical narratives were rehearsed constantly in the black community, and the black preachers developed an unusual capacity to memorize the narratives.

The Bible as the word of God formed the basis of Pennington's protest of slavery. He believed that the Bible, as the Word of God, should be applied to the existential human situation. Therefore, he sought to interpret the Bible and to show its opposition to slavery. He believed that the Bible was not neutral on the subject of slavery but bitterly against it. This was important for Pennington; his entire faith rested on this apparent stand that the Bible took on the subject of slavery. He believed that the Bible, as the inspired word of God, served as the most genuine grounds for protest of slavery. It was his contention that if he could be convinced that the Bible sanctions slavery, he would immediately look for "another book, another repentance, another faith, and another hope." Pennington implied that if the Bible sanctioned slavery, it would not be worthy of adherence for divine guidance, inspiration, and direction. He was not aware, however, of the fact that men in other ages were slaveholders and that the Bible records this; but, as Pennington perceived the issue, the question as to whether the Bible condemns or sanctions slavery was not affected by what the Bible records as historical data but only by what the Bible unveils as consistent or inconsistent with the nature of God.[4]

Regardless of the proslavery advocates and the slaveholders' effort to argue in support of slavery based on biblical history, Pennington persistently answered them by combining biblical history with the existential appropriation. When he asked, "In reference to slavery, is it consistent with the will of God?" his question had both historical and existential implications. His main concern was: Does the Bible show slavery to be right in the eyes of God? Does the Bible look upon slavery approvingly?

In response, Pennington spoke specifically of the New Testament and argued that its general tenor and scope condemns slavery. He contended that the precepts, doctrines, and teachings are against slavery.[5] He did not use the proof-text method—that is, he did not take one or a group of scriptures that condemn slavery and use either as authoritative over the rest. But his position was that a general overview of the centrality of the Bible clearly shows its opposition to slavery.

Pennington's purpose in insisting that the Bible stands in opposition to slavery was not only geared toward the freeing of black Americans from slavery, bondage, and oppression but also toward correcting and humanizing the slaveholders' distorted use of the Bible. "We make this stand, not upon the narrow question of clearing ourselves from eternal bondage; but believing, as we do, that if the New Testament sanctions slavery, it authorizes the enslavement of the whites as well as us." It is clear, at this point, that Pennington's theological method moved from particularity to universality; he started with an appropriation of the Bible in light of the existential reality of black slavery, bondage, and oppression, then moved into an appropriation of the Bible in light of its universal stand against slavery. Pennington felt that his immediate protest to the enslavement of black Americans had implications for the totality of humanity.[6] Pennington believed that the redemption of both the slaveholders and the enslaved was dependent on the protests of the enslaved and the capacity of the slaveholders to hear God's voice of protest operative in the enslaved. It would have been morally wrong for the enslaved to submit to slavery, and it was morally wrong for the slaveholders to perpetuate the institution of slavery.

Ethics

Pennington was consistent in his theology: having contended that the Bible was opposed to slavery, he then argued that it was sinful and evil to enslave another. He defined sin and evil in the context of social phenomena. He did not perceive sin as some abstract idea detached from man's function and relationship in societal institutional structures. The first ethical duty of man, according to Pennington, is to love and obey God. He based this, in part, on the scriptural passage I John 4:19, which says we love him because he first loved us. This love for God transcends all other concerns and becomes the foundation of man's commitment. One's love for God presupposes obedience. Pennington felt very strongly about the scriptural passage that says, "If a man love me, he will

77

keep my words: and my Father will love him, and we will come unto him, and make our abode with him" (John 14:23).

Since he believed that slavery was in opposition to the Bible, he did not feel that the slaveholders were Christian, because they were practicing something that was inconsistent with both God's love and the Bible. He felt that it was not enough to know God's Word intellectually; to know it in reality meant to obey it in practical situations.

> Obedience to this word, to be practical, must intend conformity to all its injunctions. This obedience must be practical, because it is made the very test of Christian character. He that would show himself to be a Christian must show it by his obedience to the Christian's statue book. [7]

Pennington took the position that this obedience to the Word of God should be esteemed above one's own opinions and above the opinions of others, however pious or eminent. "Let your motto be, what saith the Lord,—that will I do." [8] This kind of theological-ethical stand gave great momentum to Pennington's protest against American slavery. Although the American government had defined slavery as legal, Pennington argued that black Americans were not morally obligated to obey the definiton, because of its inconsistency with both God's nature and the Bible. And, since obedience to God transcended all other concerns, Pennington did not feel that anyone was committing a sin or a crime by disobeying a government that created and perpetuated an institution that was in opposition to God's will. In many instances the white church developed theological arguments in support of slavery, contending that blacks should submit to it, but Pennington argued the contrary based on an ethical mandate which transcended the white church and the American government.

78

JAMES W. C. PENNINGTON (1812 – 1871)

Salvation

Salvation for Pennington included the liberation of both the soul and the body; it was organically perceived rather than compartmentally. White ministers argued that preaching the gospel to the slaves did not include the proclamation of physical freedom. In fact, they believed that the deeper the slave's piety, the better workman he would be. They attempted to indoctrinate the slaves to believe that to accept slavery and to work hard meant to realize their rightful place in society and to ensure their seat in heaven. In other words, according to this definition, spirituality or the salvation of the soul had no implications for freedom in this world whatsoever. It meant exclusively that the slaves would get both their freedom and their reward in heaven. Pennington opposed this and contended that the gospel of Christ was concerned with the salvation of the body and the soul here on earth. "Give the slave his Bible and his ministry, who dare expound it to him, and his chains will not bind him long."[9] This gospel that Pennington referred to did not attempt to perpetuate and support slavery, oppression, and man's inhumanity to man as the white proslavery ministers did, but it called for the immediate eradication of slavery and the aspiration to achieve the complete salvation of the soul and the body. What happens after one achieves the salvation of the body and the soul? Is this an individualistic concept?

Pennington, being a fugitive slave, could have easily become insensitive to the plight of the slaves in the South. However, in the first place, his understanding of the nature of salvation would not allow him to do that. And in the second place, he did not perceive salvation as an individualistic concept but as corporate experience. He realized that his freedom was inextricably bound up with that of the enslaved blacks in the South and that the

79

northern blacks could not consider themselves free until the enslaved blacks in the South were free. This collective sense of salvation greatly enhanced Pennington's dedication and commitment to the abolition of slavery.

As a Christian, Pennington knew that he could not be apathetic and indifferent about slavery even if he wanted to. He felt that the experience of salvation was analogous to the experience that the prophet Jeremiah had when he tried to keep silent. It was the burning fire shut up in the bones of the prophet Jeremiah that made it more wearisome to him to bear than to speak the word of God. And, he described the experience of salvation as being analogous to the apostles' when against great opposition they said, "We cannot but speak the things which we have seen and heard." [10] For Pennington, salvation was an experience that forced one to be involved in the world. This involvement included speaking out against slavery and all forms of injustices.

Man

Pennington's conception of man attempted to correct the distorted definition of the black man, which emerged from the institution of slavery.

> A slave is one who is in the power of his master to whom he belongs; the master may sell him, dispose of his person, his industry and his labor; he can do nothing, possess nothing, nor acquire anything, but what must belong to his master.
> All their issue and offspring born and to be born, shall be, and they are hereby declared to be and remain forever hereafter absolute slaves, and shall follow the condition of the mother. [11]

This definition gave the black man no hope whatsoever. Everything about it was negative. Its primary goal was to keep black Americans in perpetual slavery and bondage.

80

Contrary to this, Pennington argued that black Americans were sustaining the truth of the biblical account of the origin of man. Basing his position on the Bible, Pennington said that of one blood God made all people of the earth. His theological interpretation of this biblical fact was that all people are brothers, including blacks and whites. He sought to break down ideological walls of superior and inferior races and to influence people to see that all men originate from one source. This was indeed a rude awakening for the slaveholders. It attempted to destroy the master-slave relationship and to create a person-to-person relationship. Pennington had to instill within the thinking of black Americans that, in spite of how the slaveholders perceived them, they were persons of value because they were members of God's family. They were significant, and the same God who created the whites also created the blacks. The white slaveholders and the proslavery advocates tried to indoctrinate the slaves with the belief that they were descendants of something other than the human family. But Pennington and other black Americans repudiated this claim with the realization that they were a part of the family of God as everybody else was and that in the eyes of God there are no superior and inferior persons. "Christianity teaches that all men were originally equal; that the Deity is no respecter of persons, and that all men were to give an account of their actions hereafter." [12]

Eschatology

The eschatological interpretation of James W. C. Pennington's was geared toward the total abolition of slavery and the complete emancipation of black Americans here in this life. His theory was not focused on life after death in an otherworldly, eschatological manner. It was not compensatory because it did not look for rewards in the afterlife for the pain, suffering, and oppression experienced in slavery. "We do not expect to remain in slavery; we are laying off our fetters at the rate of 2,500 annually." [13] All of these freed black Americans escaped from throughout the South where slavery existed. Pennington believed that it was morally right to assist these fugitive slaves in any way possible in order to facilitate their escape. Since slavery was condemned by the Bible and was in total opposition to the will of God, Pennington felt that it was the slaveholders who were guilty before God of a moral sin, not the fugitive slaves.

Pennington contended that the plight of black Americans toward complete freedom and liberation was preserved mainly by the desperate hope for a better day coming. This hope transcended the empirical evidences for hope. It was based on the belief that God, the author of liberty, was participating in their quest for freedom and liberation. He believed that the night for black Americans had been long, but the day was slowly dawning. In terms of his deep faith and consciousness, Pennington was able to rise above the conditions of slavery in America and to not only foresee the day when slavery would be abolished but to also foresee the day when blacks would be full citizens in America. He never accepted the idea that blacks should be deported to Africa in order to be emancipated, nor did he accept the idea that blacks should be given a section of America in which to live, but he was of the opinion that blacks had literally built America through hard work without any compensation and by enduring countless experiences of cruelty, injustice, psychologically and physically oppressive conditions, man's inhumanity to man, and all sorts of social evils; because of this, he felt that blacks should be given

82

their rightful due and become an integral part of every
aspect of American society.

> Our destiny is bound up with that of America; her ship is
> ours, her pilot is ours, her storms are ours, her calms are
> ours. If she breaks upon any rock, we break with her. We
> love America and hate slavery the more; and thus, loving
> the one and hating the other, we are resolved that they shall
> NOT LONG DWELL TOGETHER.[14]

Contribution

James W. C. Pennington was a man of unusual courage
and commitment. His theological presuppositions grew
out of the social context of slavery. He continually
reminded America that slavery was in opposition to both
the will of God and the Bible itself. He took a stand on this
issue, in spite of the possible consequences, with the
courage and faith that one's allegiance and commitment
to God transcend all other concerns, even the concern for
one's own life. He called this form of commitment "the
Christian zeal."

Ministry, to Pennington, meant involvement in the
totality of man's experiences, including both secular and
sacred experiences. He did not perceive theology or the
gospel of Christ as something concerned only with the
soul or the spiritual needs of man; it was concerned, he
believed, with the liberation of both spiritual and physical
dimensions of man. He opposed and challenged the
dichotomized interpretation of theology and the Bible that
the slaveholders and the proslavery advocates attempted
to instill in the minds of the slaves and projected an
organismic theological orientation as the norm. With this
organismic perspective, Pennington could easily understand the political, social, and educational advancement

83

and economic dimensions of society. He spoke out against slavery and all forms of social evil, not only because blacks were enslaved, oppressed, and victimized by social evils, but because of the moral principle that it is one's Christian duty to speak out against slavery and all forms of social evil on both levels of particularity and universality.

Chapter VII
Henry Highland Garnet
1815–1882

Brief Sketch of Garnet's Life

Henry Highland Garnet, like Nat Turner, was very much influenced by the Walker *Appeal*.[1] Not only did Henry Highland Garnet have great appreciation for Walker's *Appeal*, he also had great admiration for David Walker himself. It is interesting that David Walker was not a preacher, but his *Appeal* had a great effect on two of the most revolutionary preachers of the nineteenth century. Nat Turner, as we have observed, was influenced more by the *Appeal* in terms of its messianic, violent, revolutionary emphasis; and Henry Highland Garnet was more influenced by the social, political, economic, and theoretical aspects of the *Appeal*. The effect of Walker's *Appeal* on Henry Highland Garnet was evident in his famous speech delivered at the National Negro Convention held in Buffalo, New York, in 1843. The similarities and dissimilarities between the thought of Garnet and Walker will be discussed later in this chapter.

On December 23, 1815, Henry Highland Garnet was born in Kent County, New Market, Maryland. Garnet was of royal lineage; he was the descendant of an African chief from the Mandingo tribe. Garnet's grandfather was captured and sold to the slave traders who brought him to

America and later resold him into American slavery in the state of Virginia. His grandfather was later transferred from Virginia to Colonel William Spencer in Maryland.

In 1824 when Garnet was only nine years old, his father, mother, sister, seven other slaves, and Henry himself escaped to the North where he and his family finally settled in New York City. This escape from slavery was very significant in shaping the life and direction of Henry Garnet. It taught him to love freedom and to despise slavery. It also gave him a spirit of protest of slavery and oppression as well as a feeling of worth and integrity.

This feeling of protest and hatred for slavery reached a determinative point in Garnet's life when he discovered, after returning from Washington, D.C., on board a schooner as a cook, that his family were scattered by slave catchers. His father and mother escaped, but his sister was temporarily captured and was tried before Richard Piker, recorder of the New York City area. This incident was very significant in shaping Garnet into a revolutionary. He was very dedicated to his family; his family was a very close unit, and it disturbed him greatly when he returned and found them dispersed. At this particular moment the only thing that Garnet could think of was revenge upon the slave catchers. He purchased a large clasp knife and boldly walked up Broadway in the hope that some slave hunter would approach him.[2] Garnet was responding to the evils of oppression and man's inhumanity to man. This incident forced Garnet to temporarily become fixated on revenge and violent protest; it occurred in 1829 and was an experience that he never forgot.

Six years later in 1835 another incident occurred in Garnet's life that further contributed significantly to his hatred of racism, slavery, oppression, and the second-class treatment that black Americans experienced at that time. Garnet, along with Alexander Crummell and Thomas Sidney, was the first black student enrolled at Noyes Academy in Canaan, New Hampshire.[3] When the whites decided that they could not tolerate seeing blacks educated, they began to terrorize Noyes Academy in order to force the fourteen black students attending the academy to leave the state. Alexander Crummell reported that at about eleven o'clock one night a tramp of horses was heard approaching, and a rider fired past the house where the black students were living. "Garnet quickly replied by a discharge from a double-barrelled shotgun which blazed away from the window." Crummell says that the shot by Garnet probably saved their lives because the riders did not return.[4]

After leaving Canaan, Garnet resumed his studies at Oneida Institute in Whitesboro, New York, Upon his graduation from Oneida Institute in 1840 he began a school for black youth at Troy, New York, in the First Presbyterian Church. "Two years later he was ordained and installed as the first pastor of the Liberty Street Negro Presbyterian Church of Troy."[5]

Black Unity

When did black Americans begin to come together as a people and unite around a common problem? With the current interest and awakening of black consciousness, one wonders whether black unity is a recent concept. Looking into the historical situation, one discovers that black unity is not a new concept and that contemporary discussions of it are, in large measure, based on this past.

Henry Highland Garnet, along with David Walker and others, can be seen as a forerunner of black unity and the black-liberation struggle. Garnet and Walker were freemen. Garnet was born a slave and later escaped to the North and settled in New York. Walker was born free in North Carolina, left the South very early in his life, and settled in Cambridge, Massachusetts. Although they were freemen, they never viewed their future as being detached from the slaves in the South. Both saw their state and their destiny as well as the state and future of all free northern black Americans as being inextricably bound with the slaves of the South.[6]

Not only can the foundation of black unity be seen in the work of Walker and Garnet, but it can be seen in northern black Americans' formation of the annual Negro conventions. There were twelve Negro conventions that were held before the end of the Civil War. The meetings consisted of resolutions, addresses, and discussions about the social, political, economic, and educational well-being of black Americans. Although they were free, northern blacks realized that they were only nominally free and that the nation judged a man not by the content of his character but by the color of his skin.[7] The fact that the blacks saw fit to meet annually in conventions is evidence that they had a sense of unity, nationalism, and realization that the freedom of northern blacks was inextricably bound with that of southern blacks. Garnet captured this sense of unity and nationalism in his address to the slaves of the United States of America; "While you have been oppressed, we have also been partakers with you; nor can we be free while you are enslaved. We therefore, unite to you as being bound with you." Garnet referred to the fact that, not only were the slaves and the free northern blacks bound together by a common humanity, but they were bound together in terms of more tender relations such as parents, wives, husbands, children, brothers, sisters, and friends.[8]

88

Critique of Slavery

Garnet, in his famous address to the Negro slaves of the United States in 1843 at the Annual Negro Convention held in Buffalo, New York, made one of the most powerful attacks on American slavery since the Walker *Appeal* in 1829. The intent of his address was to move the slaves and the abolitionists to a new form of attack on the institution of slavery. Prior to the Annual Negro Convention movement which started in 1830 in Philadelphia, the leading antislavery tactic was moral suasion; with the creation of the convention movement, the abolitionists began to rely not only on moral suasion as a means of eliminating slavery but political tactics as well.[9] This interest in political tactics as a means of abolishing slavery became significant with the birth of the Liberty party. The party expressed their political tactics by becoming interested in the ballot, and second by organizing and developing programs and plans of direct action.

Garnet began his program of direct action by first awakening in the minds of the slaves the cruelties of slavery. He reminded the slaves that their foreparents came to America against their will. They came with broken hearts from Africa and were condemned by the slaveholders to unrequited toil and deep degradation. The first generation of Africans came to America as slaves; succeeding generations of Afro-Americans inherited their "chains, and millions have come from eternity into time, and have returned again to the world of spirits, caused, and ruined by American slavery."[10]

American slavery attempted to systematically keep the slaves on a level with animals. Intellectually every possible effort was made by the slaveholders to keep the slaves ignorant. Not only were they denied the right to go to school, but they were even denied the right to read the

Bible.[11] Culturally, every effort was made by the slave-holders to deprive the slaves of developing strong values, family ties, and a strong sense of dignity, self-respect, and self-appreciation. They were denied the freedom to participate in the institutional structures of the society that they built with their own physical strength. Garnet mentioned this in his speech delivered at the seventh anniversary of the American Anti-Slavery Society in 1840. Garnet reminded America that during the American Revolution when America herself was fighting for freedom, blacks participated in this revolution that gave America freedom and independence. Garnet pointed out that many black Americans were killed during this revolution in defense of America; and yet historians have yet to adequately give black Americans their rightful place in the American Revolution. "Yet truth will give them a share of the fame that was reaped upon the field of Lexington and Bunker Hill. Truth will affirm that they participated in the immortal honor that adorned the brow of the illustrious Washington." Having done all this for the cause of American freedom and independence and having worked daily from sunup to sundown to build America, Garnet said that blacks had earned their rightful share as citizens of America. He showed the paradox of America in that the succeeding generations of the black Americans who fought for the freedom and independence of America found themselves enslaved, imprisoned, dehumanized, and oppressed in their own land.[12]

Theology of Henry Highland Garnet

A Theology of Resistance

After providing a description and a critique of slavery to the slaves of the South, Garnet developed what can be called a theology of resistance. Like David Walker and Nat Turner, he based his idea of resistance on the Christian faith. He felt that the Christian faith, when properly interpreted, remained the most revolutionary document for resisting and overthrowing the institution of slavery. It is for this reason Garnet felt that the slaveholders prevented the slaves from reading the Bible. He gave the slaves a sense of hope and optimism in the midst of hopelessness and the pessimism of life. He said to the slaves that they would not be defeated until the slave-holders had blinded their mind's eye and had shut off the light that comes from the word of God. [13] But as long as black Americans could receive the inspiration of resis-tance from the Word of God, Garnet foresaw an ultimate victory over slavery.

The slaveholders used the Bible to condone slavery and to perpetuate it, but Garnet used it to condemn and abolish slavery. He began by saying to the slaves that it was wrong and sinful for them to submit to slavery. "TO SUCH DEGRADATION IT IS SINFUL IN THE EXTREME FOR YOU TO MAKE VOLUNTARY SUBMISSION." [14] This was indeed one of the most revolutionary statements that the slaves had ever heard. The slaveholders had succeeded in indoctrinating some slaves into believing that they were predestined to be slaves and should, therefore, willingly submit to enslavement. But the majority of the slaves did not believe that they were predestined to be slaves. It is my contention that if they had believed this they would have had no basis for hope and also would have perished in the pessimism of slavery and defeat. Those who submitted to slavery did it in protest or against their will. Rather than submit to slavery, many slaves committed suicide, and many parents killed their babies rather than have them grow up as slaves. One instance of this occurred in Covington when a father and mother, shut up in a slave baracoon and doomed to the southern market, "did by mutual agreement send the souls of their children to Heaven rather than have them descend to the hell of slavery, and then both parents committed suicide."[15]

The slaveholders and other slavery advocates said that slaves were of an inferior race and that they were content in their subordinate position; also, many abolitionists "tended to depict the Negro slave as a passive instrument, a good and faithful worker exploited and beaten by a cruel master." The picture many historians, anthropologists, sociologists, and religionists have of slaves is of docile creatures.[16] But an investigation into the facts tends to repudiate this, and Garnet's contention that it was sinful and wrong for the slaves to submit to slavery is one case in point of the slaves' resistance to oppression. The slaves were taught that it was Christian to submit to slavery and unchristian to resist it. Garnet, in opposition to this, said to the slaves that it was Christian for them to resist slavery and unchristian for them to submit to it.

In terms of their Christian duty and responsibility, Garnet charged the slaves that they were to revere and obey the commandments of God. If they did not obey God, Garnet felt that they would meet with the displeasure of the Almighty because he requires man to love Him supremely, to love one's neighbor as oneself, to keep the sabbath day holy, to study the Bible, to bring up one's children with respect for the law, and to worship no other God but Jehovah, the God of the Old and New Testaments.[17] But how were the slaves to keep the Commandments? Garnet argued that slavery made it literally impossible for the slaves to keep the commandments of God because they were not free to worship God as they pleased. They were forbidden to read the Bible; they could not assemble at will to worship God; and, they were not free to express themselves religiously. The slaveholders taught the slaves that if they were good and obedient, then they would get their reward in heaven. But Garnet said to the slaves that to remain oppressed would not assure them of heaven. He said that the slaves would not be vindicated for slavery; God was not going to reward them for having been good slaves. Since slavery made it impossible for slaves to be practicing Christians, Garnet told them that "God will not receive slavery nor ignorance, nor any other state of mind, for love, and obedience to him." [18] He said that the condition of slavery did not absolve the slaves of their moral obligation. What was this moral obligation? It was to resist slavery with all their power so that they could become free persons. He felt that to be Christians meant to be free; therefore, it was not God's will that the slaves should suffer and remain in slavery. "The diabolical injustice by which your liberties are cloven down, NEITHER GOD, NOR ANGELS, OR JUST MEN, COMMAND YOU TO SUFFER FOR A SINGLE MOMENT. THEREFORE, IT IS YOUR SOLEMN AND IMPERATIVE DUTY TO USE EVERY MEANS, BOTH MORAL, INTELLECTUAL, AND PHYSICAL, THAT PROMISES SUCCESS." [19]

Sin and Repentance

What did Garnet mean when he charged the slaves to use "every means, both moral, intellectual, and physical, that promises success"? He did not mean that the slaves should immediately resort to violence. In the tradition of the Old Testament the prophet always appealed to the moral will of the people—that is, he attempted to prick their hearts to repentance before he declared doom and destruction upon the nation. Garnet spoke of the hope of a transformation of the moral will of the oppressor first. Garnet had hoped that his address, if taken seriously by the slaves, would force the slaveholders to realize the

93

guilt and sinfulness of slavery and then repent. In 1843 when Garnet gave his "Address to the Slaves of the United States of America," he had not lost hope in the possibility of transforming the oppressors into authentic genuine Christians.

He asked the slaves to appeal to the salveholders' sense of justice and to tell them that it was wrong and sinful for them to oppress another people. Garnet charged the slaves to entreat the slaveholders to remove the grievous burdens that they had imposed upon the slaves and to remunerate them for their labor. "Tell them in language which they cannot misunderstand, of the exceeding sinfulness of slavery, and of a future judgment and of the righteous retributions of an indignant God." [20]

Garnet felt that he was advising the slaves to go through the proper channels. He believed that if the slaveholders would realize their sinfulness and repent, this would be in the interest of both the oppressor and the oppressed, as well as the nation at large. But, he said, if the slaveholders "commence the work of death they, and not you, will be responsible for the consequences." [21] Garnet meant that if the slaveholders failed to free the slaves, then the only fate of the slaveholders would be that of doom and destruction. He did not believe that God would tolerate the institution of slavery to exist forever; this is why he spoke of a "future judgment, and of the righteous retributions of an indignant God" as being the fate of the slaveholders if they did not repent. And knowing that the slaves could not become any more oppressed than they already were, Garnet said that "they had better all die—die immediately, than live slaves." [22]

Redemption

How was redemption to come between the slaves and the slaveholders? Were the slaveholders going to repent of the sin of slavery and make possible a new divine relationship with the slaves? Although Garnet appealed to the moral conscience of the slaveholders with a hope that they would repent, he wondered whether America was capable of genuine, honest repentance. Therefore, reflecting on the nature of redemption in the Bible, Garnet spoke from Hebrews 9:22: there is not much hope of redemption without the shedding of blood. [23] Thus, he anticipated the Civil War and felt that before the institution of slavery would be abolished, the blood of blacks and whites was going to be shed. He said to the slaves that if they must bleed, let it all come at once because it is better to die freemen than to live to be slaves.[24]

Garnet knew that redemption did not come easily and that the price of it was very costly. It was going to be costly for the slaves and the slaveholders. Neither the slaves nor the slaveholders could be genuine Christians until redemption came. He said to the slaves that they must act for themselves because "if hereditary bondmen would be free, they must themselves strike the blow," and the cost of redemption comes when they strike the blow they must be ready and willing to die if necessary. In this connection Garnet called for a slave strike; he said, "Cease to toil for the heartless tyrants, who give you no other reward but stripes and abuse." He felt that if every slave throughout the South ceased to labor, this would bring slavery to a rapid end. Therefore, he said, "Let your motto be RESISTANCE! RESISTANCE! RESISTANCE!"[25]

What kind of resistance was Garnet referring to? Was it physical resistance? Physical resistance was not the immediate kind of resistance to which Garnet was referring. He saw violence as the ultimatum. The slave strike itself was a kind of resistance. He advised the slaves to use expediency as the criterion for determining the kind of resistance appropriate for the particular situation. This shows that Garnet was not an innately violent man. However, he was more of a realist than an idealist. He knew that it was going to take the shedding of blood to abolish slavery, but he wanted to avoid it if possible; he even went to the extent of saying that "the Spirit of the gospel is opposed to war and bloodshed." He said in 1859 while eulogizing John Brown that he had hoped to see slavery abolished without the shedding of blood, but he saw that hope clouded with a greater form of slavery and oppression. Thus, he contended that "for the sins of this nation there is no atonement without the shedding of blood."[26] Therefore, his only hope was that if bloodshed must come, he wanted the slaves to be prepared for it.

Contribution

The life of Henry Highland Garnet was filled with the attempt to transform the social evils of society. His attempt in this regard reached its highest expression in his address delivered at the Annual Negro Convention in Buffalo, New York, in 1843. This address was indeed his most significant one, and it has had a great impact on the development of black religion, the black church, and American history. It stands alongside David Walker's *Appeal* as being among the foremost revolutionary literature produced during the antebellum period. In fact, as we have observed, Henry Highland Garnet was influenced by the theological presuppositions embedded in the Walker *Appeal* to the extent that he republished it along with his own address.

We have clearly observed that Henry Highland Garnet combined or synthesized spiritual liberation and physical liberation. In his 1843 address, he challenged the slaves to resist slavery and to use moral, intellectual, and physical

96

HENRY HIGHLAND GARNET (1815 – 1882)

means to eradicate slavery and oppression. He contended that God was in favor of this and that the oppressed had a mandate from God to resist the oppressors. It was, as Garnet perceived it, a sin to submit to slavery and oppression. He felt that one cannot be a Christian and a slave at the same time. One cannot worship God authentically, according to Garnet, in slavery.

Chapter VIII
Samuel Ringgold Ward
1817–1878

Early Life and Development

Samuel Ringgold Ward was born on October 17, 1817, in the state of Maryland. His parents were slaves; he was born a slave. Ward's parents were religious; they appropriated their religion, however, in terms of protest and resistance to slavery rather than submission to it. They did not submit to slavery because they believed that it was the work of God.[1] God, for Ward's parents, represented a reality that was opposed to slavery and oppression, and, therefore, they could not reconcile the reality of God's goodness with the evils of slavery. The only resolution they felt was adequate was to escape from slavery. Thus, they walked out of the house of bondage and "arrived on the 3rd day of August, 1826, and lodged the first night with [relatives], the parents of the Reverent H. H. Garnet." This experience had a lasting effect on the life and development of Samuel Ringgold Ward; it instilled in him a love for freedom and a resistance to slavery and oppression. For this, he felt indebted to his parents and was greatly hurt upon their death. But, on the other hand, the death of Ward's parents brought great joy. His father died in 1851, and his mother died in 1853. Reflecting upon their death, Ward said: "I felt relief from my greatest earthly anxiety. Slavery had denied them education,

98

property, [class], rights, liberty; but it could not deny them the application of Christ's blood, nor an admittance to the rest prepared for the righteous."[2]

Samuel Ringgold Ward's parents had instilled in him a deep love for freedom and a bitter resentment of slavery and oppression. After their death, he continued the quest for freedom and liberation. Ward was indeed a versatile genius endowed with superior intellectual abilities; and, fortunately, through the aid of Gerrit Smith, Ward obtained a liberal education and greatly developed his intellectual powers. He then entered the ministry and for several years was pastor of an all-white congregation of the Presbyterian Order in Butler, New York.[3] Ward distinguished himself as an outstanding preacher, orator, and lecturer. "As a speaker, he was justly held up as one of the ablest men, white or black, in the United States."[4]

Antislavery

Ward was an unusual preacher for his day because he directed his entire life's ministry to the antislavery cause. He focused his ministry organismically: he did not compartmentalize reality. He was as concerned with the transformation of social, political, economic, and educational phenomena as he was with spirituality. Thus, for Ward, the theological question was grounded in the existential situation, namely, How can the gospel facilitate the eradication of slavery and oppression? He felt that whether he was in America, abroad, on land, at sea, in public or private places, in the pulpit, or on the political platform, his labors must be antislavery labors, because his life was dedicated to the antislavery cause.[5] In fact, Ward felt that every black man, whether bound or free, should be devoted to the antislavery cause. He made no distinction between the enslaved black man and the so-called free black man. Having himself escaped from slavery in Maryland, to freedom with his parents, he had experienced both freedom and slavery. After becoming free he did not try to detach himself from those slaves who were not as fortunate as he and others, but he identified with them and devoted most of his time to their freedom.

Samuel Ward began his antislavery efforts by first attacking the American definition of the black man as an inferior being. He said that the enemies of the black man, slaveholders in particular, and white oppressors in general, denied his capacity for improvement or progress; they argued that the black man was deficient in morals, manners, intellect, and character. According to Ward, when the founding fathers developed the Declaration of Independence they felt that the black man was neither fit for nor entitled to the rights, privileges, and immunities that are granted to all men.[6] Ward realized that according to the decision of the Supreme Court of the land, blacks were not considered persons with citizenship rights to be respected. An example of this was the Dred Scott decision of 1857 which not only opened all federal territory to slavery but also denied the citizenship of the black man.

> This unfortunate class have, with the civilized and en-lightened portion of the world, for more than a century, been regarded as being of an inferior order, and unfit associates for the white race, either socially or politically, having no rights which white men are bound to respect.[7]

Ward realized that the slaveholders and white oppressors were trying to "go so far as to deny that the Negro belongs to the human family." He told of an experience involving a very learned white minister of New Haven, Connecticut, and his friend Samuel E. Cornish. The minister said to Cornish that wealth, education, nor religion could make the black man fit to live on equal terms with the white man. A white Congregational minister told Ward in the presence of A. G. Beeman that, in his judgment, "were Christ living in a house capable of holding two families, he would object to a black family in the adjoining apartments."[8]

Ward condemned these treatments of the black man as unchristian and inhuman. He condemned the white church for perpetuating these unchristian and inhuman attacks against the black man. He felt, as one Englishman did, that white Christianity could be referred to as "Negro-hating Christianity." Ward fought against these oppressive and inhuman treatments with all his might; he did it by lecturing, by holding antislavery conventions, by distributing antislavery tracts, by maintaining antislavery societies, and by editing an antislavery newspaper.[9]

Ward was critical of distinguished white northern pulpit orators who defended slavery from the Bible, using both the Old and New Testaments. He found this prevalent in most white religious denominations. Those who did not speak out in favor of slavery were silent on the matter. Ward said that if those ministers spoke out at all on the issue of slavery, they not only condemned it in the abstract but condemned the abolition of slavery in the concrete. They did not view slavery as sinful and did feel when pressed, that "some sins are not to be preached against." In opposition to this, Ward preached against slavery and challenged the white churches to take a stand against it. But because the white church was so infiltrated with slaveholders, it was difficult for Ward to significantly use it to take a united stand against slavery. During his day, Ward said that one sixth of all the slaveholders belong to Methodist, Baptist, Episcopal, and Presbyterian congregations. And, for one to condemn slavery as sinful, as Ward did, offended these slaveholders because they

101

considered themselves good Christians. They felt that they treated their slaves well, showed signs of piety, were regular in their church attendance, were pious in conversation, and were sound in doctrine. By the standards of the white church, the slaveholders were devout Christians. They denied the sinfulness of slaveholding and sheltered themselves against what they considered faults of the abolitionists. Others used the Bible to defend the institution of slavery. On the other hand, Samuel Ward and other abolitionists pointed out the intrinsic cruelty of slavery, not from an abstract perspective removed from reality, but in the concrete. They exposed slavery's injustices, sinfulness, unrighteousness, brutalizations, chattelizations, and dehumanizing utility value.[10]

Theology of Samuel Ward

God

Samuel Ringgold Ward conceived of God as a dynamic power participating in the black man's quest for freedom and liberation. He thought of God as a reality that transcended the institution of slavery and was actively engaged in its eradication through men. Ward referred to God as God of the oppressed and "God of the poor."[11] He did not perceive God as a participant in proslavery efforts. In spite of the attempt of the slaveholders and white oppressors to indoctrinate Ward and other blacks with the theory that God was interested in the perpetuation of slavery, Ward perceived God as a reality opposed to slavery and all forms of oppression and man's inhumanity to man. Since God represented such characteristics as goodness, truth, justice, righteousness, mercy, love, and judgment, Ward appealed to God for direction when he found none within the white church. He appealed for the wisdom from above which is first pure. When the proslavery advocates cautioned Ward that God has nothing to say about the social, economic, and political evils of society, Ward reminded them that spirituality and social reality are inextricably bound together. He reminded them further that the true prophets of the Old Testament and the apostles took special efforts in denouncing and rebuking all forms of iniquity.[12] Ward did not see a dichotomy between one's Christian duty and responsibility to society.

Ward showed the contrast between the conception of God of the proslavery advocates' who sought to maintain the institution of slavery and his own conception of God that sought to eradicate slavery. He repudiated the conception of God of the proslavery advocates; he felt that their God was a false God and not the God of the Old and New Testaments. Not only did he believe that the proslavery advocates were trampling the fundamental characteristics of the Christian conception of God, he also felt that the political system was corrupted and devoted to the perpetuation of slavery. The political system of America had departed from the Constitution which it created and which contended that no man shall be deprived of liberty without due process of law; the constitution also sought to secure freedom and liberty for all mankind. At this point, the effort of Samuel Ringgold Ward was to force the political system of America to include blacks in the Constitution and the Declaration of Independence. In other words, when the Declaration of Independence says, "We hold these truths to be self evident that all men are created equal and that they are endowed with certain inalienable rights that among them are life, liberty, and the pursuit of happiness," Ward insisted that this also referred to black Americans. What Ward and the abolitionists wanted was simply the application of the Declaration of Independence to blacks as well as whites and that both should secure the benefits of the Constitution. But to accomplish this, voting was required.

Ward and other abolitionists lost faith in the Democratic and Republican parties; rather than working toward the eradication of slavery through political action, both parties worked for its perpetuation. Ward could have become indifferent about black political participation since things seemed rather hopeless, but instead he joined the Liberty party which was organized in 1840 in Syracuse, New York, on antislavery principles. Henry Highland Garnet was also very active in the Liberty party. Ward casted his first vote with this party and devoted all his political activities to it.[13]

Fugitive Slave Law, Ethics, and Eschatology

In September of 1850, the fugitive slave law was passed; this law not only endangered the freedom and liberty of the fugitive slave but free blacks of the North as well. Prior to the fugitive slave law, if slave catchers abducted an alleged fugitive and if the alleged fugitive slave could prove that he or she was a free person by law, the slave catchers had to let the person go free; but the fugitive slave law made all this void. On the basis of a slaveholder's affidavit presented before a judge or commissioner, an abducted fugitive slave was not even given a jury trial. After the fugitive slave law of 1850, the official's fee for finding a fugitive slave guilty was ten dollars, and five dollars if the person was not guilty. This law also required residents to prevent accused fugitive slaves from escaping.[14] The black man's response to the fugitive slave law of 1850 was one of militance and pessimism.

On the basis of Samuel Ringgold Ward's participation in the Liberty party, and on the basis of his continued quest for freedom and liberation for all black Americans, it became very evident that he was optimistic of the possibility for the actualization of this freedom and liberation. It is clear that Ward's "aim seemed to be not so much to preach the gospel of heaven as to preach the gospel of this world that men calling themselves Christians might learn to respect the natural and political rights of their fellows."[15] And, obviously he believed that there was genuine hope for this possibility, but the fugitive slave law of 1850 forced him to take a second look at this possibility even to the extent of encouraging militancy and pessimism. This is not to say, however, that he lost all faith in America and completely resorted to an otherworldly eschatology.

It is important to note that in spite of the pessimism of the fugitive slave law of 1850, Ward continued the fight for black liberation, realizing the possibility that he might have to use a different method. He was of the opinion that America, in the passing of the fugitive slave law of 1850, demonstrated an insensitivity to moral suasion as a means of achieving freedom and liberation. What was the black man to do in this situation? How was he to respond ethically? What was his moral duty? Was he to submit to this unjust law that was created by unjust men for unjust reasons? Or, was his moral duty to change the law? Ward described the law as despotic because it was made by despots for despotic purposes. It destroyed the integrity of the black man, his house, his personhood, and his right to life, liberty, and property.[16] Ward argued that the black man's response to this unjust law should be militant protest, not one of submission.

Samuel Ward contended that since the fugitive slave law of 1850 stripped black Americans of all manner of protection by the writ of habeas corpus, jury trial, or any process known to civilized man, it threw black Americans back upon the natural and inalienable right of self-defense and self-protection. The basic question for black Americans, as Ward perceived it, was whether they "will submit to being enslaved by the hyenas which this law creates and encourages, or whether [they] will protect [themselves]."[17] What alternative did the fugitive slave law of 1850 give black Americans? From Ward's perspective, it gave them the alternative of dying as freemen or living as slaves. This feeling is captured in the words of the song:

> Oh freedom! Oh freedom
> Oh freedom, I love thee
> And before I'll be a slave
> I'll be buried in my grave
> And go home to my Lord
> And be free.

This willingness to fight for one's freedom even at the cost of life rather than submit to slavery did not stop with the death of Samuel Ward, nor with the death of the antebellum slaves. Claude McKay, a poet of the Harlem Renaissance era, wrote of this determination.

> If we must die, let it not be like hogs,
> Hunted and penned in an inglorious spot
> While around us bark the mad and hungry dogs,
> Making their mock at our accursed lot.[18]

Ward reminded the slaveholders and the white oppressors that the fugitive slave law which made it legal to catch slaves and kidnap freemen was nothing more than

106

open warfare on the rights and liberties of the black men of the North; and to enlist in that warfare was certain, immediate, and inevitable death and damnation. Many black Americans had a similar response to this law. Echoes of protest and resistance came from blacks at Brooklyn, Williamsburg, the Portland Convention, and Philadelphia.[19] Frederick Douglass responded by saying that "the only way to make the Fugitive Slave Law a dead letter is to make half a dozen or more dead kidnappers. . . . The man who takes the office of a bloodhound ought to be treated as a bloodhound." Henry Highland Garnet carried a pistol, and it is reported that Samuel Ward said, "Although the law might try to enslave every Negro in New York there was still one Samuel Ward—who will never be taken alive."[20] Ethically, the issue of the fugitive slave law of 1850, as Samuel Ringgold Ward, Henry Highland Garnet, and Frederick Douglass perceived it, was one of survival. They felt that the slaves would be forced to defend themselves if the slave catchers attempted to capture and enslave them. They began to question the viability of moral suasion as a tactic for the eradication of slavery and oppression.

Contribution

Samuel Ringgold Ward was one of the most distinguished and outstanding black clergymen of the nineteenth century. He achieved distinction as a great preacher, lecturer, thinker, and exponent of the abolitionist movement. Many people of his day referred to him as "the black Daniel Webster"; he always spoke with eloquence, creativity, and well-developed ideas. "From 1840 up to the passage of the Fugitive Slave Law in 1850," Ward traveled extensively, lecturing in every church, hall, or schoolhouse in western and central New York on the abolition of slavery and the inalienable rights of black Americans.[21]

He dedicated his entire life to the cause of freedom and liberation. Being a fugitive slave himself, he knew what it meant to be oppressed; therefore, he sought to utilize all his abilities in the total elimination of the institution of slavery. Although he became pastor of an all-white church in South Butler, New York, he did not let his antislavery activities suffer. For his ultimate goal was working toward the development of a society here on earth in which people could relate to one another as persons rather than as things. He challenged every political, economic, social, religious, and educational institution that condoned or encouraged the institution of slavery. Christianity, the gospel of Christ, and theology made up the foundation of Ward's protest against the violent forces of slavery and oppression. He felt that the centrality of the gospel was a call for the freedom and liberation of all mankind and that this should represent the direction of the Christian church. Thus, Ward was opposed to any attempt to separate the Christian gospel, theology, and the church from social, educational, political, and economic involvement in the world. He interpreted the Christian ministry from an organismic perspective rather than a bifurcated perspective. This is why Ward, as a clergyman, was so outspoken against social evils.

Samuel Ringgold Ward was a man of great courage, perseverance, and religious commitment. He was not afraid to take a stand on an issue, regardless of its consequences. In spite of the passing of the fugitive slave law of 1850, and in spite of the tremendous support that the social, economic, political, educational, and religious institutions gave to that law, Ward boldly took a stand against it and condemned it as an act of oppression, slavery, man's inhumanity to man, and barbarism.[22] Indeed this took great courage and strength. He said that there were as many northern senators in support of the fugitive slave law of 1850 as southern senators.

Chapter IX
Alexander Crummell
1819–1898

Early Life and Development

Alexander Crummell was born of free parents on March 3, 1819, in New York. His father, Boston Crummell, was a descendent of the very tribe that used to dwell at the region of Timanee, West Africa, now known as Liberia. Unlike many black children of that day, Alexander Crummell was able to go to school and to become eventually a very learned man. His education was made possible in part by his parents who were concerned with the total well-being of young Alexander. He first attended what was then referred to as Colored School Number One, which was on Mulberry Street in New York City. In 1831, he enrolled in the Canal Street High School, which was founded by Peter Williams, Theodore Sedwick Wright, and the Tappan brothers. He enrolled in that institution along with Henry Highland Garnet, and they became lifelong friends. Crummell became the protégé of Theodore Sedwick Wright, and Garnet became the protégé of Peter Williams; both Crummell and Garnet excelled their benefactors in the pulpit, writing, oratory, and international distinctions.[1] After Crummell had learned all that the Canal Street High School had to offer, he along with Garnet and Thomas S. Sidney journeyed from New York to Canaan, New Hampshire, to attend Hayes Academy. Hayes Academy was founded in 1835 by abolitionists of

110

New Hampshire who were "disgusted with the Negro-hatred of the schools, and mortified at the intellectual disabilites of the black race."[2] Thus, together, Alexander Crummell, Henry Highland Garnet, and Thomas Sidney began the long and difficult journey from New York City to Hayes Academy in Canaan, New Hampshire. Crummell said that on the steamboat from New York to Providence, Rhode Island, they had no cabin passage because none was allowed to blacks.

On the steamboat, not only did they not have a cabin, but because of their color they were denied food and beds. After arriving in Providence, Crummell pointed out that "coaches then were in use, and there were no railroads"; therefore, for many miles from Providece to Boston, from Boston to Concord, from Concord to Hanover, and from Hanover to Canaan, the three of them were forced to ride night and day on the top of the coach. The journey was indeed filled with pain, suffering, hunger, and affliction. "It was a long and wearisome journey, of some four hundred and more miles; and rarely would an inn or a hotel give [them] food, and no where could [they] get shelter." Crummell said that he could not forget the difficulties of his trip; the sufferings from pain, sufferings from exposure to the cold weather, sufferings from thirst and hunger, and sufferings from taunts and insults at every village, town, and farmhouse. He then found it hard to believe that Christians could thus treat human beings in such an inhuman manner. They finally arrived in Canaan with the expectation of remaining there for a long time, only to be shocked with the realization that "the Democracy of the State could not endure what they called a 'Nigger School' on the soil of New Hampshire." Therefore, word went forth, particularly from the politicians of Concord, that Hayes Academy must be closed; they could not conceive of blacks' getting a decent education. There were fourteen blacks enrolled at Hayes Academy, and as the result of it, the entire state of New Hampshire became panic-stricken.[3]

The farmers of Canaan united, and on the fourth of July they decided to remove Hayes Academy as a public nuisance; on the tenth of August they came together and "seized the building, and with ninety yokes of oxen carried it off into a swamp about a half mile from its site." And, at about eleven o'clock one night a group of night riders approached the boarding house where Garnet, Crummell, and Sidney were staying and fired at it. "Garnet quickly replied by a discharge from a double-barrelled shotgun which blazed away through the window."[4] Crummell said that the musket shot by Garnet saved their lives. They immediately left New Hampshire and returned to New York City to discover that Oneida Institute at Whitesboro, a manual-labor seminary, had opened its doors to blacks. Their thirst for learning continuing, Crummell, Garnet, and Sidney enrolled at Oneida, spending three years under the instruction of Beriah Green. Crummell and Garnet graduated from Oneida Institute in 1839. Garnet then immediately entered public life, and Crummell applied for admission to General Episcopal Theological Seminary in New York City. His application was made in the form of a petition to a committee of which Bishop Onderdonk of Pennsylvania served as chairperson. Crummell's admission was denied although he qualified in every way but color.[5]

In spite of Crummell's rejection by General Episcopal Theological Seminary, he studied persistently and mastered the courses of instruction that he would have gotten at that seminary. He was admitted to the deaconate in the Massachusetts diocese on May 30, 1842, by Bishop Griswold and was later raised to the order of priesthood by Bishop Alfred Lee of Delaware. Crummell then journeyed to Philadelphia and applied for admission to Bishop Onderdonk's diocese. Although he had with him a letter of introduction from Bishop Griswold, his admission was denied. He then engaged in mission work in New York City. In 1848 Crummell visited England for the purpose of raising funds for his mission work. While he was there he attended Cambridge University, graduating with a B.A. degree. He then returned to New York City for a short visit, after which he sailed for Liberia, West Africa, arriving there on July 15, 1853, to work as a missionary. He spent twenty years as a missionary in Liberia and Sierra Leone.[6]

Theology of Alexander Crummell

God, Providence, and Evil

Alexander Crummell did not conceive of God in an abstract metaphysical sense, detached and removed from the course of human events. In fact, he was very critical of any attempt to compartmentalize God and to separate him from history. He said, "I know indeed that there is a piety (so called) which would fain convince us that the God of the Bible has nothing to do with the profane histories of men."[7] He ascribed this position to the philosophy of Manichaeanism, which contended that the world was dualistic. This dualistic cosmology found its expression in the idea of the world's being controlled by two independent forces—the force of evil and the force of good. God was believed to be the head of good, and the devil or Satan was thought of as the head of evil. Crummell could not accept the philosophy of Manichaeanism, because it left "the moral evils of the world to the disposal of some other great being besides God." Also, he could not accept it because it not only removed God's

113

involvement from the affairs of man but negated God's omnipotence and sovereignty as well. Crummell repudiated this notion of two independent powers controlling the world and argued that there was one sovereign, overruling Being who governs all things in both heaven and earth and directs the course of history by his own independent power.[8]

The background of Crummell's cosmology is a biblical influence; and from this he was led to an organismic conception of the world as opposed to a bifurcated one. The world was not split into two realities for him but constituted an organismic whole, with God residing at both transcendent and immanent levels. In his immanence, God is a dynamic, active, ever-present, moving force in the world. His involvement included both sacred and secular dimensions of existence. And, his immanence, for Crummell, meant that there was nothing in the world removed from God's domain and control. Crummell argued that God's omnipotent hand interpenetrated the totality of history and that the animating spirit of history was the very breath of God.

If God directs the totality of history, as Crummell suggests, then how does he account for evil in the world? How did evil originate? From the Manichaeaistic perspective, it is very easy to account for the presence of evil in the world, in that it is an independent power controlled by Satan or the devil; it stands alongside the power of good. It is also in opposition to the good. Because of his organismic conception of reality, Crummell could not explain evil in a dualistic manner. He accounted for evil not as independent and alongside God but rather as a power under God's domain and control. Crummell did not conceive of God as the originator of evil but as the power that controls it. "For while indeed God is not and cannot be the author of evil, still he is Governor of the wicked, and exercises a masterful authority over their works and ways." [9] Crummell believed that God never allows evil to run unchecked, to have its own uncontrolled career, and to do as it pleases. Thus, God constantly checks and limits evil's activity and intentions. "Whenever [God] sees wrong, He steps in and interferes, to turn it some way into good." [10] Crummell firmly believed that history attests to the claim that God takes evil and transforms it into good. He asks, if God does not take evil and transform it into good, then how can we account for the many marked incidents in history when from apparently disastrous causes have emerged positive results?

Attempting further to support his claim, Crummell points to the history of the nation Israel. The Israelites did not just happen to settle in Egypt by chance, but their presence there grew out of the providential events of God connected with the sale of Joseph by his brothers, which was an evil act. [11] But from this act Joseph eventually became a ruler in Egypt and was able to save his family and Israel itself from starvation. In response to the evil act of his brothers, Joseph said, "So now it was not you that sent me hither, but God" (Gen. 45:8). The idea that Crummell propounded was not that God creates or wills evil but that he uses it in the achievement of his goal. Taking the omnipotence of God seriously, Crummell realized that God, if he chose to do so, could eradicate evil. And, since God did not choose to eradicate evil totally, Crummell concluded that God permits evil to prevail in the world. Does this kind of thinking justify the presence of evil in the world? If God chooses to use an evil act for his greater good, does this condone the act? Does this make the person committing the act justified before God?

Crummell struggled with these hard questions in relating his theory of providence to the plight of black

Americans for freedom and liberation. However, his answers to these questions are not satisfactory because he views the enslavement of black Americans on the one hand as retributive and on the other hand as restorative.[12] By retributive, in a sense, Crummell believed that the enslavement of blacks in America was the result of previous sins. He argued that our forefathers in remote generations committed the sin of not glorifying God as the real God, and they did not like to retain him in their knowledge. Thus, from generation to generation our ancestors became more and more removed from the true God, resulting in the omnipotent God permitting the cruelest of evils to devastate Africa and to carry off its people into foreign slavery.[13]

Crummell's idea of providence and his concept of divine retribution must be examined critically at this point. Certainly his theory of providence is inadequate in that it totally frees the oppressors and slaveholders from all feeling of guilt and responsibility for the enslavement of black Americans. Following Crummell's thinking, God used the slaveholders as his instruments for punishing his people. This not only condones slavery but makes it an evil that black Americans brought upon themselves. Also Crummell's theory of providence must be viewed critically because of its obvious ethnocentricism. He considers only the Christian conception of God as the real God; for him the God of traditional African religions was not real but was a god of paganism.[14] He did not realize, however, that the God of traditional African religions predates the emergence of Christianity in Africa. In West Africa, where the bulk of slaves came from, and the portion of Africa to which Crummell referred, the Christian notion of God was almost unknown until the Portuguese and Spaniards started missions in the area during the sixteenth century.[15] Having been educated in the European tradition at

116

Queens College of the University of Cambridge, England, where the Christian notion of God prevailed, Crummell projected the ideal theistic model and said that it was God's will for Africans to govern themselves accordingly. He wanted to impose the Christian religious tradition on the African religious tradition.

His theory of providence and divine retribution was too heavily grounded in biblical analogies. Without regard for biblical criticism and with the gap between the historical events of the biblical community and the existential situation of black Americans, Crummell spoke as though God punished black Americans for forsaking him in the same manner that he punished the nation Israel. He was very much influenced by Jeremiah 25 which tells of the seventy years' captivity of Israel and of the succeeding destruction of Babylon. His point was that as God allowed Israel to be held captive, so did he allow black Americans to be enslaved. "And the exiled children of Africa, in distant lands, were made an astonishment, and an hissing, and perpetual desolations."[16]

The restorative aspect of Crummell's theory of providence focused on the regeneration and evangelization of Africa. He felt that upon coming to America, black Americans were reunited with the true God and, therefore, were prepared to return to their homeland to Christianize it. He contended that at the close of three centuries of slavery, millions of the sons and daughters of Africa in the United States were "turned from the paganism of their fathers; the people that sat in darkness have seen a great light."[17] Through their suffering and oppression, Crummell felt that God redeemed the injured slaves and scourged their oppressors; and as a result, tens of thousands of black Americans became enlightened from books, seminaries, the Bible, and churches. At the end of God's providential plan, Crummell continued, hundreds of Africans would return to Africa as colonists, merchants, missionaries, catechists, and teachers to evangelize and regenerate Africa.[18]

> I feel as if I could laugh to scorn all the long line of malignant slavetraders who have defiled and devastated this wretched coast of Africa, and fling in their teeth the gracious retort of Joseph: "As for you, ye thought evil against us, but God meant it unto good, to save much people alive.[19]

From Crummell's theory of God's restorative plan and from the above quotation, it becomes even more apparent that his position has many discrepancies. In addition to my criticisms of Crummell's theory of providence, let me speak strongly to its inviability and untenability: if black Americans had believed that their slavery was predestined by God or was the result of God's providential plan, they would not have had grounds to resist slavery and to fight for its eradication. The dominant thinking among the slaves was not that slavery was the result of God's providential plan but rather that it was in direct opposition to God's plan; and because they believed this, they were able to resist and oppose slavery. To resist and oppose slavery meant to conform to the will of God. As an ex-slave remarked:

> You charged me that in escaping I disobeyed God's law. NO indeed! that law which God wrote upon the table of my heart inspiring me to love freedom, and impelling me to seek it at every hazard, I obeyed and, by the good hand of my God upon me I walked out of the house of bondage.[20]

The prevailing concept of providence among the slaves was that slavery was in direct opposition to the will of God and that the slaves should not submit to it but reject it.[21]

118

ALEXANDER CRUMMELL (1819 – 1898)

Man, Ethics, and Eschatology

Alexander Crummell was a systematic thinker; his theological ideas hinged on his theory of providence. His concept of man can best be understood when viewed from the background of providence; the same applies to his concept of ethics and eschatology.

He began his doctrine of man by making it clear that because of his belief that the slavery of black Americans was the result of providence, it did not mean that God had placed black Americans under a curse. In fact, he argued that the act of slavery of black Americans was not peculiar to them as a people but was a part of the general social evil existing among the whole human family. "In God's providence, the Negro family have latterly been called to suffer greatly, and doubtless for some high and important ends."[22] Crummell felt that because black Americans survived slavery, succeeded in all areas of life in spite of the systematic attempt of the slaveholders to dehumanize them, it meant that there was something superior about the black man. Many other races, Crummell continued, would have perished under the same kind of oppressive conditions that blacks were forced to encounter. Crummell was of the opinion that God had chosen the black race for some great purpose, which was the redemption of both Africa and America.[23] In his conception of man, Crummell first affirmed the black man in terms of his personhood, divine chosenness, and historical significance. He then perceived God's providential plan's being worked out through the black man. These two aspects show the particularity and universality of Crummell's conception of man.

Crummell defined man as a social being—that is, man exists in community, society, institutional structures, and social phenomena. Man possesses an innate quality that

119

motivates him toward a group existence rather than an individual existence, detached from community. Man is gregarious. Crummell applied this sociological fact to the black man and to humanity at large. He viewed the family concept as the foundation of gregariousness: on the one hand, the black community he perceived as a family, and on the other hand, he considered mankind in general a family.[24] Each race, in this sense, constitutes a family. In America there are many races or families of peoples, but Crummell was particularly concerned with the black race and the white race. The problem for Crummell was, Can man be conceived in such a way as to break down the polarization between blacks and whites? Crummell then asked the question in another manner: Will amalgamation or absorption eradicate the race problem between blacks and whites in America?[25] Underlying the theory of amalgamation was the idea of the black race in America loosing their color identity and becoming dissolved into the white race. This theory was entertained by some during the nineteenth century because of the realization that color was a handicap to blacks in America.

Crummell, however, rejected the theory of amalgamation on the grounds that it went against the evolutionary process of nature. He contended that nature moves in an evolutionary process from the simple to the complex, "starting off in new lines from the homogeneous to the heterogeneous, striking out in divers ways into variety."[26] Despite the genetic improbability of amalgamation, Crummell felt that it was undesirable because it would force the black race to negate itself in terms of what God would have it to be. He argued that all races should accentuate themselves at the maximum capacity and actualize their potentialities. They should realize their differences, accept one another for what they are in spite of their differences, and function on an interdependent basis, thus enabling the black race to become what it has the capacity to become without oppression and slavery, and likewise for the white race. Crummell believed that this would break down the polarization between blacks and whites, and it would also redefine the race problem in America. As he perceived it, the race problem was not a problem of amalgamation, but it was a moral one.[27]

When Crummell referred to the race problem as a moral one, he was referring to ideas and principles that are first conceptual and then applicable. In other words, the question of morality for Crummell concerned itself with both theory and practice. He felt that the task of resolving the moral question was to begin with ideas and principles that are grounded in theory and then to appropriate them according to the social, political, and economic situation. "The race problem is a question of organic life, and it must be dealt with as an ethical matter by the laws of the Christian system."[28]

Crummell's ethics should be interpreted according to his theory of providence: What is man's ethical duty in regard to resolving the race problem in America? What is the ethical imperative for both black Americans and white Americans? Based on his theory of providence, Crummell believed that God works on the basis of certain times in history. History, therefore, was thought of as teleological—that is, goal or purpose directed. Things were not thought of as happening by chance; everything happened for a purpose. Thus, in realizing one's ethical imperative, one must recognize the timelessness of an occasion before acting, so as to assure oneself that one is acting with God; this guarantees the success of the consequences of an ethical decision. "But it is to be observed in the history of man that, in due time, certain principles get their set in human society, and there is no such thing as successfully resisting them."[29] The rise of these principles is not by chance but represents God's hand in history. The principles represent the providence of God, and no earthly power can detain them.[30] He felt that the time for the deliverance of the black race had come, and nothing could prevent it from happening.

Crummell argued that two of these moral principles are brotherhood and democracy. Both represented the truth of God's reality. Brotherhood referred to a universal concept that sought to authenticate man; the spirit of democracy does not deride God and authority on the one hand and crush the weak and helpless on the other hand, but it upholds the doctrine of human rights, demands and protects honor of all men, recognizes manhood in all conditions, and uses the government as the agency for the unlimited progress of humanity. He felt that democracy when defined in this way has its foundation in the scriptures of God. "The democratic principle in its essence is of God, and in its normal state it is the consummate flower of Christianity, and is irresistible because it is the mighty breath of God."[31] When properly understood and practiced, Crummell thought that democracy was the solution to the race problem in America and was the ideal form of government.

What direction did Crummell perceive as the eschatological pilgrimage of black Americans? Did he lose all faith and hope in America and view Africa as the paradigm for black liberation? At best, the eschatology of Crummell concerning black liberation considered the perspective from both Africa and America. He did not abandon all hope in America and resort to a total commitment to the liberation of Africa, and he did not believe that all blacks should leave America and return to Africa. "And indeed, the deportation of the whole Negro race, in this land, is not a necessity, nor a requirement."[32] Why would Crummell make such a statement? Because he firmly believed that God's providential plan was for the regeneration of Africa; but in order to accomplish this task, God only needed "remnants" of black Americans to return to Africa. He contended that it is by remnants that God achieves the goals of providence and grace; he referred to these as "the elect" or the "chosen few." In this context Crummell was committed to Africa and called upon black Americans to return to Africa to regenerate and strengthen it in every way, including such developments as religion, agriculture, politics, economics, education, and the like. He was greatly committed to this task and said to black Americans that it was their moral and Christian duty and responsibility to return to Africa to rebuild and regenerate it.[33]

On the other hand, Crummell called for the total freedom and liberation of blacks in America. In reference to the race problem, Crummell argued that America was on trial, and the black man is the only solution. In other words, on the basis of the black man, America stands or falls. "If the black man cannot be free in this land, if he cannot tread with firmness every pathway to preferment and superiority, neither can the white man."[34] For he believed that as a bridge is never stronger than its weakest point, so it is with man. A nation is never stronger than its most oppressed members.

> "In nature's chain, whatever link you strike,
> Tenth or ten-thousandth, breaks the chain alike."[35]

So closely knitted, inextricably bound, and interwoven is humanity that "the despoiling of an individual is an injury to society."[36] Humanity as an ideal universal norm transcends any ethnic particularity. When ethnic classes perish, humanity continues to live. Humanity, said

Crummell, as a universal norm, anticipated the multiplicity of ethnic varieties and has a place for all of them; but as a principle and concept it rides above them, outlives them, and swallows them up in terms of duration. The democratic concept, therefore, in terms of its essence and authentic meaning is the highest expression of humanity because it comes from God. Moreover, America, as it stands before God and attempts to resolve the problems of racism, slavery, oppression, and man's inhumanity to man, according to Crummell, has a divine mandate to be truly democratic. What will happen if it does not?

> If this nation is not truly democratic then she must die. Nothing is more destructive to a nation than an organic falsehood! This nation cannot live—This nation does not deserve to live—on the basis of a lie!
> Her fundamental idea is democracy; and if this nation will not submit herself to the domination of this idea—if she refuses to live in the spirit of this creed—then she is already doomed, and she will certainly be damned.[37]

As we have observed, the eschatology of Crummell is grounded in concrete reality, the physical world. He believed that man's quest for freedom and liberation should be focused in this life and that man's ethical responsibility was to challenge political, social, educational, and economic oppression, to make the kingdom of God become a living reality here on earth. His eschatology, however, does not exhaust itself in this-worldly thought. He possessed a dual eschatological interpretation. There was a realm of reality beyond this world—that is, man was perceived as living in two realms. The realm of transcendence consisted of eternity, infinitude, inexhaustibility, immutability, absoluteness, perfection, and changelessness. These ideas represented norms or paradigms for man's ethical and eschatological pilgrimage on earth.[38] These norms were used by Crummell to critically evaluate existence in terms of its temporality, finitude, exhaustibility, mutability, relativity, imperfection, and changeability; thus making his otherworldly eschatology functional within his this-worldly eschatology. For example, Crummell felt that "perfect humanity" was a universal abstract metaphysical norm which took on concrete tangible existential reality in terms of ethnic variety; the same applies to such concepts as justice, peace, love, virtue, and mercy. These ideas in their absolute objective essence came from God and are available to man for actualization.

Contribution

Alexander Crummell's contributions to the struggle of black liberation in both Africa and America are indeed vast and diverse. He distinguished himself in Africa and America as an outstanding orator, lecturer, preacher, educator, and missionary. He was a missionary in Africa for twenty years, from 1853 to 1873; while there he served in many capacities throughout Liberia. While stationed in Africa, Crummell made several visits to America. He perceived his mission in Africa as a sojourn, not as a permanent residence. As one of his many contributions to Africa, in 1866 he began his services with the College of Liberia as a teacher. He served as a minister of an Episcopal church in Monrovia. Upon returning to America in 1873, he settled in Washington, D.C., and organized the St. Luke's Protestant Episcopal Church.[39] This church immediately became one of the leading churches of Washington, D.C., with Crummell serving as minister for several years.

The last year or two of his life were spent around his

birthplace in New York. Because of his love for and dedication to black Americans, he started the American Negro Academy in 1897 with the intention of laying the foundation for an institution that would preserve the history and achievements of blacks in both thought and action. The desperate need for such an institution was the constant theme of Crummell's later years.

Chapter X
Edward Wilmot Blyden
1832–1912

Early Life and Development

Edward Wilmot Blyden was born in St. Thomas, Virgin Islands, in 1832. He was born of free literate parents. His mother was a schoolteacher and his father was a tailor. In 1842 Edward and his family moved to Puerto Cabello, Venezuela, for two years. After returning to St. Thomas, Blyden became acquainted with John P. Knox who later became his mentor. Because of the influence that John P. Knox had over Blyden, he later decided to enter the ministry. In 1850 Blyden came to the United States and attempted to enroll in several theological seminaries but was denied admission because he was black. Not only did Blyden experience racial discrimination in his quest for education, but he witnessed all sorts of racial evils because of the fugitive slave law. This made him realize that free blacks in the North were in an oppressed situation similar to that of the enslaved blacks in the South. The fugitive slave law endangered the freedom of northern blacks as well as those in the South. The slave catchers would come from the South looking for fugitive slaves and would, in many instances, catch any black person and return him to the South as a slave. Becoming convinced very quickly that there was no hope for genuine black liberation in America, Blyden began to make plans for a trip to Africa. He accepted an offer from the New York Colonization Society to defray his expenses to Liberia. Thus, on December 21, 1850, Blyden sailed aboard the *Packet Liberia,* arriving in Monrovia, Liberia, on January 26, 1851. [1]

In Liberia, Blyden did not waste any time but immediately became active in preparation for leadership. He attended high school in Monrovia and was trained to be both a teacher and clergyman by D. A. Wilson, who was a graduate of Princeton Theological Seminary. Blyden proved to be an exceptional student. He studied theology, the classics, geography, mathematics, and many other subjects. In 1858, Blyden was ordained a Presbyterian clergyman, and during the same year he succeeded D. A. Wilson, his mentor, as principal of Alexander High School. He did not stop here but continued to advance in distinction and achievement. In 1862, he was appointed professor of classics at Liberia College. He combined his professorship at Liberia College with a position as secretary of state in President Warner's administration from 1864 to 1866. And in 1880, he was appointed president of Liberia College.[2] As president of Liberia College, Blyden began to think in terms of launching a Pan-African program, using the college as the point of departure. He thought of it as an instrument to assist in the development and ongoingness of Pan-Africanism to intellectual ends, for social purposes, in religious duty, for patriotic arms, and for racial pride. From Liberia College he felt that blacks could advance further and become one with the great tribes on the African continent.[3] Blyden's goals and aspirations were geared solely toward the development of Africa rather than toward black liberation in America.

Christianity,
Slavery, and Pan-Africanism

Blyden was very critical of the slaveholders' perverted use of Christianity and viewed it as another reason that blacks in America should return to Africa, the homeland, rather than seek freedom and liberation in Africa. He points out that many of the African slaves who became members of the Christian church were taught that it was their duty "to submit, in everything, to their masters."[4] This was taught by the church, clergymen, and slaveholders; it was written in books used for the instruction of the slaves. The slaves were instructed on the basis of "oral tradition" because they were not allowed to learn to read. Blyden mentioned a book written by William Mead, who was then Bishop of the diocese of Virginia, and whose book of sermons for slaveholders was published. In the book, Bishop Mead pointed out that God made slave masters and mistresses to take care of their children. He said that this same God made servants and slaves to work for their masters. According to Blyden, Bishop Mead also said that it pleased God to make blacks slaves and to give them nothing but poverty in this world. Thus, whenever a slave master saw the need to correct a slave, Bishop Mead said that it was the slave's moral duty to submit to the slave master whether he deserved the punishment or not.[5] The Bishop was not alone in his feelings; they were also shared by magistrates, legislators, clergymen, governors, property owners, mayors, presidents, and professors of theology—"all united in upholding a system which every Negro felt was wrong."[6] What was the response of black Americans to this perversion of the Christian faith?

Although much of the religion of black Americans was taught to them by slaveholders and oppressors, they did not accept it in the manner in which it was taught. They rejected the distorted, perverted, and oppressive interpretation of Christianity and sought a more genuine and authentic view of Christianity. This view said to them that slavery was in total opposition to the will of God, therefore, making it their moral duty to resist and protest slavery and all forms of oppression. In spite of the afflictions, pain, cruelty, injustice, unrighteousness, and pessimism of slavery, black Americans were able to find inner peace and to aspire for a better future. Because they discovered this inner peace and hope for a better future in this world, "in the hours of the most degrading and exhausting toil, they sang of the eternal."[7] The Jews were not able to sing by the waters of Babylon. They said in Psalm 137:1-4:

> By the rivers of Babylon, there we sat down, yea, we wept, when we remembered Zion. We hanged our harps upon the willows in the midst thereof. For there they that carried us away captive required of us a song; and they that wasted us required of us mirth, saying, Sing us one of the songs of Zion. How shall we sing the Lord's song in a strange land?

But black Americans in the midst of the dungeon of slavery, oppression, and man's inhumanity to man were able to make themselves instruments of music and to sing the sweet melodies of Zion. This, however, did in no way mean that they were happy with their condition. It means that they found peace within themselves in spite of the evils of slavery. And at the same time, they fought against slavery with everything possible.

Theology of Edward Blyden

Providence and Pan-Africanism

It was Blyden's contention that slavery of any kind was an outrage, because "it spoils the image of God as it strives to express itself through the individual or the race."[8] He believed that God dwells within man, therefore making man a part of God. Being influenced by the words of Paul, "For in him we live, and move, and have our being" (Acts 17:28a), Blyden argued that it is through God incarnated in us that we have the freedom to act out ourselves. Thus, if any man lives, moves, and has his freedom in God, then God will live, move, and have his freedom in man. Slavery prevents both God and man from acting out this freedom.

God, for Blyden, was organismically conceived; he felt that a distinct phase of God's character was set forth to be wrought into perfection in everything. This principle applies to both man and nature. Each thing or person represents a variation of God's beauty and thought. In each individual person and in each race of people, a portion of God's absoluteness is realized but never exhausts itself at any point in history. Blyden perceived the whole of mankind as a vast representation of God. Therefore, man cannot extinguish a race either by conflict or amalgamation without seriously affecting God. Each person and each race, Blyden said, should have the opportunity to be free and to maximize the divinity within. Slavery does not allow persons to do this. Whenever a person enslaves another or whenever one race enslaves another, Blyden said that the enslaved should cry out in protest. "This is why the Hebrews cried to God from the depths of their affliction in Egypt, and this is why thousands and thousands of Negroes in the South are longing to go to the land of their fathers."[9] Blyden was very pessimistic about the future of black Americans in the United States. Even after emancipation he remained doubtful about the possibility of achieving black liberation in America. In fact, he felt that the advantages enjoyed by black Americans in the United States toward the attainment of manhood, since emancipation, were hardly greater than that which was attainable during slavery.[10] On the one hand Blyden views slavery as being evil and against God's nature; on the other hand, he sees it as God's instrument. How does he relate the latter to black Americans?

Blyden begins with the scriptural passage Deuteronomy 1:21, which says, "Behold, the Lord thy God hath set the land before thee: go up and possess it, as the Lord God of thy fathers hath said unto thee; fear not, neither be discouraged." He interprets this scriptural passage existentially to mean God's call to black Americans, the descendants of Africa, to go up and possess their homeland, Africa. Why not possess America? In response he said, "It ought to be clear to every thinking and impartial mind, that there can never occur in this country an equality, social or political, between whites and blacks." On what empirical grounds did Blyden make this statement? He made it on the grounds that whites are in control in America. During Blyden's day, all the political, social, economic, and educational institutions were controlled by whites. They made and administered the laws. They were teachers in the schools; they owned all the stores; they owned and controlled the banks, property, mass media, and transportation system. Blyden did not believe that whites were going to relinquish any of their power to black Americans. And, because of this, Blyden called upon blacks to return to Africa, their fatherland.[11]

There was even a greater reason that Blyden called upon blacks in America to return to Africa. He believed that it was an act of God's providence. God, he believed, was speaking to the blacks in America through the institution of slavery. He believed that God suffered black Americans to be enslaved so "they could receive a training fitting them for the work of civilizing and evangelizing the land whence they were torn." Blyden

132

was referring to the Christianization of Africa. He was committed to the Christian faith and felt that Christian black Americans should return to Africa and proclaim the gospel of Christ. According to Blyden, one of the positive things that came out of slavery was the introduction of black Americans to Christianity. In one sense Blyden argued that slavery was against the image of God in man. He was not saying that it was right but, rather, that God used the evils of slavery toward the accomplishment of an ultimate goal—the evangelization of Africa. Not only did he contend that God suffered black Americans to be enslaved, but in spite of all the services black Americans rendered to the United States, God suffered them to be treated as aliens and strangers, "so as to cause them to have anguish of spirit, as was the case with the Jews in Egypt, and to make them long for some refuge from social and civil deprivations." Blyden regarded slavery as God's providential call to all black Americans to go up and possess Africa, the land that God prepared for them. This was not a figurative utterance for Blyden. It was a literal statement and had a literal meaning. He firmly believed that God was saying to the black man of America in reference to Africa, "Behold, I set the land before you, go up and possess it." [12]

The call of providence, as Blyden perceived it, was not a call for "black power" but "African power," an African nationalism. He felt that black Americans would never receive the respect and honor of others until they established a strong, powerful nationalism. He argued that black Americans should return to African states, establish and maintain institutions, make and administer laws, erect and preserve churches, develop governments, make ships and navigate them, teach in schools, control the mass media and the economy. Blyden conceived of nationalism as an ordinance of God and, therefore, a part of God's providential plan for all races.[13]

He called upon blacks in America, from the East, the West Indies, South America, and the uttermost parts of the world to come and take part in developing a nationalism in Africa, using Liberia as the point of departure. "Liberia, with outstretched arms, earnestly invites all to come." The call was one of urgency. It was for blacks to leave the countries of their exile, as the Israelites went forth from Egypt, taking with them their trades, treasures, arts, intelligence, and skills of all sorts to be used to build a nationalism.[14] At this point, it appears that Blyden was interested in building the same kind of nationalism in Africa for the descendants of Africa that whites had developed in America. However, although the nationalisms might appear to be similar, in Blyden's intention they were very different. For he indicated that "the work to be done beyond the seas is not to be a reproduction of what we see in this country." He believed that the work to be done in Africa required the unique and peculiar perception of the descendants of Africa. It was not going to be an imitation of the American society, and, as he puts it, nor will it be the healing up of a sore wound but "the unfolding of a new bud, an evolution."[15] He perceived it as the development of a new side of God's character and a new dimension of mankind. Blyden contended that every race has something unique to contribute to the world.

Man

Blyden began his conception of man by denouncing the view held by the slave power-structure in America that blacks were less than human or that blacks were quasi-human, animals, born and destined to serve a superior race, the white race.[16] The general ethos of America was that if a black man wanted to amount to anything, he had to aspire to be like a white man. To be a black man was to be nothing. The white power-structure defined blackness as the negation of selfhood, and whiteness as the affirmation of selfhood. In opposition to this view, Blyden maintained that black Americans were not inferior to any other race and that they are capable of development and progress just like other races. In other words, blacks are in no way less capable of success and accomplishment than any other race, if they are given adequate conditions conducive to intellectual growth, stimulation, and motivation. Blyden argued that blacks are significant because they are made in the image and likeness of God. He viewed all races as possessing some unique divine quality that should be developed. Since God made all races of one blood, Blyden said that each race should have the opportunity to develop its potentialities. Not only does every race have a particular purpose to contribute to humanity, but, according to Blyden, every person has something unique to contribute to humanity. In terms of race, Blyden was a pluralist. Rather than defend the idea of one race as superior or inferior against another, he maintained that all have possibilities to be developed. The problem that Blyden saw with black Americans is not that they are inferior but that they were denied the opportunity to develop and become what they have the potential of becoming.

He continually argued, in an effort to instill racial pride, that to be African or a descendant of Africa was not negative but positive. And to give it up would mean to give up the peculiar glory to which we are called. He was very critical of those Africans who were blind to the significance of race so as to say, "Let us do away with the sentiment of race. Let us do away with our African

135

personality and be lost, if possible, in another race."[17] Blyden's response to this was that it was as impossible to do away with race as to do away with gravity, heat, cold, rain, and sunshine. Not only did Blyden view this as impossible, but he contended that to do away with one's personality meant to do away with oneself.

Blyden coined the phrase *"African personality"* to connote a corporate sense of selfhood. It was used as a wholistic phrase that referred to both black Americans and Africans; both represented one race. He urged Africans to honor and love themselves as a race because they are a great race. He firmly believed that if they refused to be themselves and tried to surrender their personality, they would then have nothing to give to the world. For racial peculiarities, he continued, are given by God. God created them for his own glory. Therefore, to get rid of these peculiarities would mean to get rid of the link that binds one to God. God's intention was that each race would be different from the rest of mankind. And this difference reveals a phase of God's character that is not granted to other races.[18]

Eschatology

Blyden believed that the entire experience of blacks in America was a part of God's plan. In fact, he felt that everything in both the physical and spiritual dimensions of reality proceeds on the basis of some great plan or order. It was his position that God's moral law regulated the movements of mankind and that all activity in both mankind and nature tends to move upward. It moves toward the highest and best results, therefore, making its outcome inevitable.[19] Applying this principle to race, Blyden constructed an eschatology that viewed Africa as "the Promised Land." Africa was the land that God had prepared and set before black Americans as he prepared and set Canaan before the Israelites. His vision of the future was to behold black Americans', the descendants of Africa, return to the "fatherland" and to rebuild it. This would reclaim the land, raise it from the slumber of ages, and rescue it from stagnation. "And then to the astonishment of the whole world, in a higher sense than has yet been witnessed, Ethiopia shall suddenly stretch out her hands unto God." [20]

Contribution

Edward Wilmot Blyden was one of the most prominent black men of the nineteenth century. He was very versatile and had a wide range of experiences. Although he was born in the Virgin Islands, most of his life was spent in Africa. After his failure to be admitted into theological school in America in 1850, he immigrated to Africa, where he was educated and became committed to Pan-Africanism. He only returned to the United States to visit eight times. He held many key positions in Africa, such as Liberian educational commissioner to Britain and the United States, Liberian commissioner to the United States to recruit blacks back to Africa, professor of classics at Liberia College, Liberian secretary of state, principal of Alexander High School in Harrisburg, Liberia, and president of Liberia College. There are also other important positions that he held.

He was committed to black liberation, but unlike the other thinkers that we have studied, he felt that it was impossible to achieve liberation in America. He compared the experience of blacks in Africa with that of the Israelites in Egypt. As the Israelites were exiled in Egypt, he felt the blacks were exiled in America. And as God called upon the Israelites to go up and possess the land of

Canaan, he contended that God was telling black Americans to go up and possess Africa, "the homeland." In his thinking, all this was an act of providence and could not have been avoided.

Although Blyden was critical of slavery and felt that it prevented the portion of God in man from developing, to conceive of God and providence in the manner in which he did, ultimately makes God responsible for slavery. He was responsible in the sense that he suffered and permitted black Americans to be enslaved. If God suffered and permitted this, then does it not mean that he could have avoided it? It has to be that he could have avoided it because of his omnipotence. Blyden believed that through slavery and suffering, God was preparing black Americans for the task of rebuilding Africa. This made their suffering redemptive in that it was unmerited. The questions, then, are: Why did God choose blacks for this task? Could he have accomplished the task of rebuilding Africa without making black suffering a prerequisite? And, does this not tend to glorify suffering? What oppressors stand guilty before God for enslaving blacks, if it was God's will that blacks be enslaved?

I raised the above questions to point out some of the problems with Blyden's conception of divine providence. For to employ Blyden's model means that the oppressor becomes God's evil instrument to accomplish a greater good. When the prophet Jeremiah foretold the seventy years' captivity of Israel and the succeeding destruction of Babylon, who did God use to accomplish this task, and how did God refer to him?

> Behold, I will send and take all the families of the north, saith the Lord, and Nebuchadnezzar the king of Babylon, my servant, and will bring them against this land, and against the inhabitants thereof, and against all these nations round about, and will utterly destroy them, and make them an

astonishment, and an hissing, and perpetual desolations. (Jer. 25:9)

We can see at this point that providence was a weak aspect of Blyden's theological position. It leaves too many questions unanswered. I feel that it is not a viable theological position. In opposition to it, slavery should be viewed as an evil act solely resulting from man's decision; in this way, man becomes responsible for slavery and not God. It was solely the white man's decision to enslave blacks, and he was not being used as God's instrument. They were acting out their own demonic intentions. This model attempts to maximize man's freedom in relationship to God. Man cannot be truly responsible for an act if he does not have the freedom to accept or reject it. God's providential plan then becomes understood in light of a movement toward man's actualization of his maximum potentialities. For me, the realization of these possibilities is not planned in advance by God. But it happens existentially as man decides to accept or reject the possibilities as they come from God.

Chapter XI
Henry McNeal Turner
1834–1915

Early Life and Development

Although Henry McNeal Turner was born of free parents on Feburary 1, 1834, in the vicinity of Newberry, Abbeville, South Carolina, because of economic reasons he was forced to work for a plantation owner alongside slaves. Turner and his parents were free, but they had difficulty competing economically with the slave labor-system. Therefore, in his childhood, Turner worked on a plantation as a blacksmith and carriage-maker. His royal lineage did not prevent him from having to experience the evil effects of slavery at an early age. David Greer, Turner's maternal grandfather, having been brought to South Carolina as a slave, was later manumitted by demonstrating to a colonial court that he was the son of an African prince and was thus entitled to his freedom. The English law at the time forbade the enslavement of Africans of royal blood, and South Carolina at the time was part of the British colony.[1]

Turner could not attend the public schools of South Carolina because after 1835 it was against the law for blacks to attend school in the state, and it was illegal for blacks to learn to read and write. However, Turner was determined to obtain an education. He displayed his interest in education by securing a spelling book; later, a white woman, a white playmate, and a black man instructed him in reading and writing. But because of the illegality of teaching blacks to read and write in the state, his instructors were forced to discontinue having sessions with him. This in no way stopped Turner's determination to learn to read and write. He soon mastered the spelling book on his own and from there began to read the Bible. Practicing reading and spelling with the Bible, Turner had completely read the Bible five times before he was fifteen years old. He also practiced memorizing long passages of the Bible, thus strengthening his capacity for memorization, which greatly aided him throughout his life.[2]

This unusual capacity for memorization was helpful to Turner when he became employed in a law firm at the age of fifteen in Abbeville, South Carolina. Because of his brilliance and commitment to learning, the lawyers at the firm took an interest in Turner and assisted him in acquiring books. He was able to read books in arithmetic, history, geography, and astronomy. He had access to legal records in the law firm and therefore was exposed to issues related to politics, which he found to be helpful in later years. In spite of the law at the time in South Carolina forbidding the education of blacks, the lawyers provided personal instruction to Turner. This enabled Turner to greatly increase his ability to read and write.[3]

Turner was converted to and instructed in Christian service by plantation missionaries. The Methodist Episcopal Church, South, admitted him as a probationer in 1848. He became converted in 1851 under the influence of a sermon preached by Samuel Leard.

> You, at Sharon Camp Ground, in 1851 so stunned me by your powerful preaching that I fell upon the ground, rolled in the dirt, foamed at the mouth, and agonized under conviction till Christ relieved me by his atoning blood. . . . I

141

have preached and worked for God in every position held from the day I gave you my hand up to the present.[4]

During the same year, Turner was licensed by an exhorter in the Methodist Episcopal Church, South, and was licensed to preach in 1853. He then for five years traveled through South Carolina, Georgia, Alabama, Louisiana, and Missouri as a missionary preaching both to slaves and to free blacks.[5]

It was not until 1857 in New Orleans that Turner became acquainted with the African Methodist Episcopal Church through Willis R. Revels, a black physician and preacher of the A.M.E. Church. Turner immediately joined. He was then recommended by the St. James Quarterly Conference to the Annual Conference of St. Louis, Missouri, in 1858. This conference was presided over by Bishop Daniel A. Payne. Turner attended this conference, preached a trial sermon, passed a rigid examination, and was admitted to the itinerant ministry of the A.M.E. Church. This event was Turner's beginning of fifty-seven years of active ministry in the A.M.E. Church.[6]

Theology of Henry McNeal Turner

God, Providence, and Evil

Turner conceived of God in a way that attempted to make his existence existentially relevant to black liberation. The important thing for Turner was not what God is in his objective essence but his meaningfulness for man. He felt that he could best understand the significance of God in light of "blackness." He approached the question of God out of the context of the black experience; therefore, his contention was that God must identify with the black man and must be symbolized in like manner. He

142

did not mean that God exhausts himself in blackness. As God identified himself with blacks, Turner argued that other ethnic groups should perceive God in light of their ethnicity. He said, "Every race of people since time began who have attempted to describe their God . . . have conveyed the idea that the God who made them and shaped their destinies was symbolized in themselves."[7] On the basis of this, Turner asked the question, Why should the Negro not believe that he resembles God? He concluded that God was a Negro. This was important to Turner because the general ethos of his day was that blackness symbolized the devil and whiteness symbolized God.[8] He was in opposition to this polarization and bitterly protested any attempt of whites to degrade blackness.

Many whites made a mockery of Turner's portrayal of God as black. But Turner reminded them of their portrayal of God as a fine-looking, symmetrical, and ornamented white man. He said, for the majority of whites believe "that God is a white-skinned, blue-eyed, straight-haired, projecting-nosed, compressed-lipped and finely robed white gentleman, sitting upon a throne somewhere in the heavens."[9] Turner criticized those blacks who were indoctrinated into believing that God was white and challenged them to perceive God in light of their own unique, existential blackness.

Turner believed very firmly in the omnipotence and sovereignty of God. He felt that God "rules in the armies of heaven and among the inhabitants of the earth."[10] This model views the totality of the world as being under God's rulership and control, and because of it, everything is interpreted as being a part of God's providential plan for the world. Does this mean that evil is condoned and justified as being a part of God's providential purpose?

And, if God controls the totality of the world, then how do we account for the presence of evil? Also, how do we account for human freedom and responsibility? Turner had to account for the evils of slavery and oppression in light of the omnipotence, intrinsic goodness, love, righteousness, and justice of God.

He began by saying that slavery was a providential institution and not a divine institution. For him, a providential event is a temporary and contingent event; a divine event is an immutable and eternal event. Any event that is divine, Turner perceived as being "as eternal as any attribute belonging to the godhead." [11] Based on his theory of providence, Turner realized that the institution of slavery was not final, nor was it ultimate. It was an evil that he believed God suffered to be. Based on his belief in the omnipotence of God, Turner knew that God could have prevented the enslavement of blacks. However, because God chose not to did not make Turner feel that he was responsible for slavery. Turner argued that whites were solely responsible for slavery. It was totally their decision, and God did not will it upon blacks. In other words, Turner did not believe that God predestined blacks to be slaves. This is why Turner contended that slavery was not a divine institution and that it could not last forever. "When the Negro was being captured, and brought to this country and subjected to a state of unrequited servitude, [God] knew the horrors of their past and present condition and foresaw . . . the termination of their slave ordeal." [12] When the time had fully come for the eradication of slavery, there was nothing anybody could do to prevent it because, according to Turner, its eradication was an act of God's providence. If it were God's providential plan that slavery be abolished, then how could slavery itself have been an act of providence? Turner answers this question in his doctrine of eschatology.

144

HENRY McNEAL TURNER (1834 – 1915)

Eschatology

Turner's experiences in America and Africa are clues to understanding his eschatology. He was converted to Christianity very early in life and became an articulate spokesman for the Christian faith. He believed that God's providential plan was to Christianize Africa. Therefore, he felt that in spite of the evils of slavery, it exposed the descendants of Africa to Christianity in order that they might become equipped to return to and Christianize Africa. For he said, "God knew that the slave regime, although exceedingly pyrotechnical at times, was the most rapid transit . . . to Christian civilization for the Negro." [13]

At one time Turner was very committed to working for the freedom and liberation of blacks in America. This is evident in many ways. Although he was a freeman, with gladness and great joy did he celebrate the emancipation of the slaves. He described it as a time of times and said that nothing like it would ever happen again. [14] Turner's commitment to freedom and liberation for blacks in America can be seen in his outstanding political career.

Because he successfully participated in the organizing of freed slaves for the Republican party of Georgia, Turner was elected to the state legislature from Macon, Georgia. He was denied a seat in the legislature because he was black, but he delivered a famous speech entitled "The Eligibility of Colored Members to Seats in the Georgia Legislature" in bitter protest of their decision. After being dismissed from the Georgia legislature for a brief period, Turner served as the first black postmaster in the state of Georgia and also as customs inspector in Savannah, Georgia. [15] He experienced racial prejudice in both positions. He also experienced much racial prejudice when he

145

was appointed the first black chaplain in the army. These negative experiences along with many others made Turner very pessimistic about the possibility of blacks' achieving complete freedom and liberation in America.[16] As an alternative, he began to concentrate on Africa as the eschatological future for blacks in America.

Shifting to Africa as the eschatological promised land for black liberation, Turner argued, "I am taking the ground that we will never get justice here, that God is, and will [continue to] withhold political rights from us, for the purpose of turning our attention to our fatherland."[17] Turner made a complete turn from an emphasis on America to a thoroughgoing thrust toward Africa. He became so negative about America that he concluded that there was nothing for blacks to aspire to in America. Blacks should, therefore, return to Africa where a black government is already in existence and where human life is sacred. Turner argued that there was nothing in America for the black man to learn or to attain.[18]

Turner's interest in Africa as the hope for the liberation of blacks in America was primarily focused on Liberia as a refuge from American slavery and oppression. He visited Africa in 1891, 1893, 1895, and 1898 but expressed an interest in the emigration of American blacks to Africa much earlier. In 1866 Turner addressed a letter to William Coppinger, secretary of the White American Colonization Society in Washington, D. C., expressing the position that blacks will never get justice in America and that God does withhold and will continue to withhold political rights from blacks for the purpose of turning their attention to Africa, the fatherland. He further stated that he had become a convert to the idea of the emigration of blacks to Africa and expected to advocate it thereafter. Turner was first influenced to the emigration idea by hearing a speech delivered by Alexander Crummell in Israel Church, Washington, D.C., on May 6, 1862.[19] After his converted belief in emigration to Africa, Turner dedicated his life to the fulfillment of his eschatological dream of total freedom and liberation for the black man in Africa. He believed that the black man could find his true manhood only in Africa.

Man

True manhood for Turner meant the realization of one's authentic identity with himself and God, and one's capacity for full participation in societal institutional structures. The ethos of Turner's day was that the black man was inferior in every respect. It said that the black man was supposed to stay out of politics, economics, and education, because of his inferiority. Turner's life represented a complete opposition to this position. Speaking of black political participation, he asked, "If the Negro is a man in keeping with other men, why should he be less concerned about politics than any one else?" He believed that for the black man to stay out of politics meant for him to reduce himself to less than man. Thus, defining true manhood, Turner said, if the black man is to be a full and complete man, he must be able to participate in everything that belongs to manhood. And, if the black man is deprived of a single duty, responsibility, or privilege, it is to that extent that he is limited and incomplete.[20] Prior to his support of emigration to Africa as the solution to the problem of being black in white America, Turner advocated the full and complete participation of blacks in American society.

When Turner was elected to the state legislature from Macon, Georgia, the white legislature refused to permit the seating of black representatives. Turner stood before the General Assembly on September 3, 1868, and delivered an address entitled "Speech on the Eligibility of Colored Members to Seats in the Georgia Legislature" in defense of his manhood and the dignity of black people. He began by informing them of his position—namely, that he was a member of that body and was not going to stoop or beg for his rights, but, rather, he said, "I am here to demand my rights, and to hurl thunderbolts at the men who would dare to cross the threshold of [his] manhood." He expressed the concern that the racism manifested in the General Assembly was unparalleled in the history of the world and that from his day back to the day when God made man, no analogy for it could be found.[21]

He said to the General Assembly that the great issue before them was a question of his manhood. He asked, "Am I a man? If I am such, I claim the rights of a man." He called upon them to stop degrading black manhood by not allowing blacks complete political participation. But because the racism of the General Assembly was so ingrained, in spite of Turner's appeal they insisted upon denying blacks the right of political participation. Turner reminded them that great societies such as Babylon, Greece, Nineveh, and Rome were destroyed because of oppression. He said that every act that man commits is like a bounding ball. If one man curses another man, that curse rebounds upon the first man; if a man blesses another man, that blessing is returned; and when a man oppresses another man, the oppression also will return. He then asked the assembly, Where have you ever heard of millions of blacks' being governed by laws yet having no part in the decision-making process? He reminded them that political systems or governments derive their just powers from the consent of the governed, and then he asked, "How dare you to make laws by which to try me and my wife and children, and deny me a voice in the making of these laws?" Because the General Assembly refused to recognize the true manhood of the black man and because of other similar experiences that Turner had, he concluded that there was no future for blacks in America. He felt that a black man might succeed in developing a livelihood in America in generations to come, "but he can never be a man—full, symmetrical and undwarfed." [22]

Contribution

The contributions of Henry McNeal Turner were vast. He made a landmark in the annals of church history and black history. His theology was grounded in the quest for freedom, justice, righteousness, and truth. He was committed to the unending task of black liberation. His theology did not gear itself toward a fixation with heaven or an otherworldly eschatological hope. In fact, in his writings Turner very seldom used the word *heaven*; and when he did use the word *heaven* it was in comparison with this world. He believed that men should live in heavenly places in this world. This is why he gave his life to the eradication of injustice, man's inhumanity to man, oppression, unrighteousness, and all sorts of social evils. He did not do this in the attempt to better prepare man for heaven. He did it so that man could become what God wants him to be here on earth.

He did not perceive the church as an entity unconcerned and removed from the world. He viewed the church as the vanguard of social, political, educational, and economic involvement in the world. His own life was a testimony to this fact. Although he spent fifty-seven years as a minister in the A.M.E. Church, this did not significantly detract from his active involvement in politics and African emigration. Because the black community was in dire need of his services both in the secular and the sacred areas of life, Turner ably served in both capacities. He did this not only because he was needed but also because of his commitment to a certain theological orientation—namely, a holistic approach to reality. He was as concerned with the secular conditions of man as he was with the sacred.

Turner served as the first appointed black army chaplain and was later reappointed a chaplain in the army and sent by Secretary Stanton to Georgia to work in the Freedman's Bureau. However, because of severe racism and the desperate need of his talent in the A.M.E. Church in Georgia, Turner resigned. He began to organize and develop that Georgia church. At that time the A.M.E. Church had only one church and congregation in the state of Georgia. The name of the church was St. Philip's A.M.E. Church of Savannah, Georgia, and A. L. Standford served as minister.[23] Turner served his church well in Georgia, and throughout the United States and Africa. Because of outstanding services for his church, Turner was elected to the highest office in the church, that of bishop. But as was said earlier, this did not prevent Turner's involvement in other areas.

He was a constant contributor of articles and statements to the *Christian Recorder,* an A.M.E. weekly newspaper. He founded and edited "The Southern Recorder," "The Voice of Missions," and "The Voice of the People." Upon his death in 1915, W. E. B. DuBois remarked:

He was a man of tremendous force and indomitable courage. As army chaplain, pastor and bishop he has always been a man of strength. He lacked, however, the education and the stern moral balance of Bishop Payne. In a sense, Turner was the last of his clan: Mighty men, physically and mentally, men who started at the bottom and hampered their way to the top by sheer brute strength; they were the spiritual progeny of ancient African chieftans and they built the African church in America.[24]

Chapter XII
Marcus Garvey
1887–1940

Early Life and Development

The African dream of Crummell, Blyden, and Turner did not end when they died; it continued and reached its peak with the emergence of Marcus Garvey. Eleven years before the death of Crummell, twenty-five years before the death of Blyden, and twenty-eight years before the death of Turner, Marcus Garvey was born on the island of Jamaica on August 17, 1887, to Sarah and Marcus Garvey. Because of the success of Crummell, Blyden, and Turner, the philosophy of Pan-Africanism was prevailing in America at the time of Garvey's birth, but at that time no one knew that young Garvey would develop it even more. Garvey's mother wanted to call him Moses because she believed he was destined for some great task.[1]

Garvey spent most of his youth in Jamaica where he was involved in a printers' union strike. After the strike proved unsuccessful, Garvey began working for the Jamaican government printing office and shortly thereafter became editor of his first publication, "The Watchman."[2] His interest in publications led him to start a newspaper called *La Prensa*, which only lasted a few months. He then began to travel, visiting Costa Rica, Bocas-del-Toro, Panama, Ecuador, Nicaragua, Honduras, Colombia, and Venezuela. Prior to returning to Jamaica, he visited London, England, and attended lectures given at Berbeck College, University of London. While in London he made use of the many available library facilities, reading everything he could find on black history and culture.[3] Here he read for the first time the autobiography of Booker T. Washington, *Up From Slavery*. After finishing it he asked, Where is the black man's government? Where are his king and kingdom? Where are his president, his country, his ambassador, his army, his navy, his men of big affairs? Garvey realized that these were not available in the black community and then vowed that he would help to make them materialize. This marked the beginning of his nationalistic consciousness on a large scale. Although the Pan-Africanism of Crummell, Blyden, and Turner significantly helped to shape the thought and direction of Garvey, it was Booker T. Washington who first inspired Garvey toward black leadership.[4]

With great enthusiasm for the illumination and the conscious awareness of the need for black leadership, Garvey left London on July 15, 1914. He had seen the black man being kicked around and oppressed in the West Indies, in South and Central Americas, and in London but was determined that he was going to do something about it. He then envisioned a new world of black men that he would lead toward the redemption of the black race, and humanity in general. Five days after arriving in Jamaica, Garvey founded and organized the Universal Negro Improvement Association and African Communities (Imperial) League for the purpose of uniting all the black people of the world into one great body to establish a country and government of their own. The purpose Garvey had in choosing this name was to include all black humanity.[5]

When Garvey started his organization he received strong opposition from the Jamaicans. Some said, "Garvey

153

is crazy; he has lost his head. Is that the use he is going to make of his experience and intelligence." One reason the Jamaican blacks immediately opposed his organization was because of his usage of the term *Negro*. Since it was fashionable to use the term *colored* when referring to blacks, many bitterly resented the usage of *Negro*. In spite of this strong opposition, Garvey succeeded in establishing his organization in Jamaica with the assistance of a Catholic bishop, the governor, Sir John Pringle, and William Graham.[6]

After his success in Jamaica, Garvey explained his plan to Booker T. Washington. He invited Garvey to America and promised to go on a speaking tour with him to enhance his work; but Booker T. Washington died in the fall of 1915, and Garvey was not able to get the full benefit of his services. However, Garvey followed through in his plans and arrived in America on March 23, 1916. Garvey went to Tuskegee to pay his respects to the late Booker T. Washington and then returned to New York City where he organized the New York division of the Universal Negro Improvement Association. He was immediately elected as president of the organization, and under his able administration, it grew by leaps and bounds.

The rapid growth of the Universal Negro Improvement Association was greatly facilitated by Garvey's origination of a paper called *The Negro World*. He served as editor of the organization's paper free of cost. He traveled throughout the United States for the organization and by 1919 had organized about thirty branches in different cities. Because of his writings and speeches, in 1919 the membership of the organization was over 2 million, and it was at this time that Garvey launched the program called The Black Star Line.[7]

On June 27, 1919, Garvey incorporated The Black Star

Line of Delaware, and in September he obtained a ship. The inclusion of The Black Star Line as a part of the Universal Negro Improvement Association added great momentum to the organization. By August, 1920, over 4 million had joined The Universal Negro Improvement Association, and during the same month a convention of black people from around the world was held in New York City. The Universal Negro Improvement Association and The Black Star Line had acquired for Garvey international distinction, and during the first international black convention over twenty-five thousand packed Madison Square Garden on August 1, 1920, to hear Garvey speak.[8] At this point Garvey and his back-to-Africa campaign began to draw international recognition and fame.

Garvey and Africa

As we have observed, Booker T. Washington's program and ideas were very influential in helping Garvey to realize the need for black leadership. However, when Garvey began to launch his back-to-Africa program he had to part company with his teacher. Garvey felt that the program of Booker T. Washington's was primarily geared toward the development of industrial opportunity for the black man in America. But Garvey believed that if Washington had lived, the changing social, educational, economic, and political conditions of the black man in America would have forced him to develop a new program. The new program that Garvey envisioned was not one of maintaining accommodation in America but of a movement from America to Africa.

The program of The Universal Negro Improvement Association and The Black Star Line was not directed

155

toward seeking freedom and liberation for blacks in America; it was directed toward a mass movement of taking blacks back to their homeland Africa. Garvey contended that blacks were strangers in America and were children of captivity. As children of captivity, he argued that blacks looked forward to a new day when they would possess the land of their fathers, the land of refuge, the prophets, the saints, and the land of God's crowning glory. He said that blacks should gather together their children, treasures, and loved ones, and, like the children of Israel who by the command of God left Egypt and went to Canaan, the promised land, blacks should leave America and return to Africa, their promised land. Garvey felt that the black race and white race were competitive and could not live permanently side by side without friction and trouble; the white race wanted a white America and the black race wanted a black Africa. Garvey did not want social equality in America between blacks and whites. He wanted to have a nation owned, determined, and controlled by blacks so that blacks could reestablish a culture and civilization exclusively theirs.[9]

Garvey believed that Africa was the legitimate moral and righteous home of all blacks. He argued that blacks and whites would learn to respect one another if they ceased to be competitors in the same country for the same things in politics and society. By having independent countries, he firmly believed that blacks and whites would be friendlier and more helpful toward each other because "the laws of nature separated them to the extent of each and every one developing by itself." Garvey called for this right to be practiced and the desire to be instilled in blacks to govern and rule themselves without fear of being encumbered and restrained. "We form a majority in Africa and we should naturally govern ourselves there. No man can govern another's house as well as himself."[10]

156

In his strong emphasis on black Americans' returning to Africa, he clearly indicated that his program was not based on hate toward whites. He said that the Universal Negro Improvement Association was organized for the purpose of enhancing the condition of blacks industrially, commercially, socially, religiously, and politically. He said, "We are organized not to hate other men, but to lift [blacks] and to demand respect of all humanity."[11] He believed that his program was righteous and just. He, therefore, declared that Africa must be free and that the entire black race must be emancipated from bondage and that Africa be made their homeland. Garvey made every effort to build his program on religious principles.

Theology of Marcus Garvey

God

Garvey conceived of God in a way that facilitated the goals and aspirations of the Universal Negro Improvement Association—namely, the independence and redemption of Africa. For Garvey the objective essence of God was colorless in that he was conceived as a spirit. But in terms of the existential appropriation of God, Garvey argued that God for blacks must be conceived as "the God of Ethiopia, the everlasting God—God the Father, God the Son and God the Holy Ghost."[12] Garvey's main concern was to demythologize the black man's conception of God and to redefine God in light of Pan-Africanism. He did not see how blacks could be true to the cause of black liberation's adhering to a conception of God that emerged from the white community. He felt that blacks should view God through the black experience and that whites should view God through their own experience. To view God, as Garvey argued, through the black experience did not mean that God literally becomes black. But it meant that when blacks view God, he takes on the identity and particularity of the black experience.

Garvey did not think of God as a passive, uninvolved reality. He viewed God as a God of both war and peace. God becomes a God of war, he continued, when man transgresses his power and interferes with his authority.[13]

He believed that as long as man worked in the interest of justice, righteousness, and the improvement of his race and humanity, God was on his side. But to accomplish this Garvey realized that man had to assert himself and make use of power. The black race in America was powerless in terms of independence and self-determination. In the attempt to help the black race realize their potential, Garvey told them that God was on the side of the powerful and the strong.[14] By this he meant that blacks must become strong and powerful as a race, and by so doing God would work in their behalf.

Man and Providence

Did God create any superior and inferior races? Garvey responded negatively to this question and asserted that God created all men equal, regardless of their color. Black people, white people, yellow people, and all other people were created as equals. Therefore, for any race to feel that they could not accomplish what another race had accomplished would be an insult to the almighty God who created all races equal.[15]

It was Garvey's contention that God made man lord and ruler of the earth. Since every man was given this responsibility, Garvey felt that whether man was white, yellow, brown, or black, nature had provided a place for each and every one. Garvey referred to geographical location: "If Europe is for the white man, if Asia is for the brown and yellow man, then surely Africa is for the Black man." He compared the black man's quest for nationhood with that of other nations, saying that the white man fought for the preservation of Asia, and blacks should be willing to shed blood for the redemption of Africa and the emancipation of blacks everywhere.[16] He believed that every race must find a home because this was what God intended. The Jews found Palestine; the Irish found Ireland; the Indians found India; and he saw Africa for the Africans.

For Garvey, God did not create any man or race without a goal or purpose in mind. He created every man with possibilities for achievement, and for man to think that he was created only to be what he is and not what he has the possibilities of becoming is to misunderstand God's reason for making man. Why did God create the black man? Did he create him to be a slave? Garvey answered in the following manner: "God Almighty created us all to be free. That the Negro race became a race of slaves was not the fault of God Almighty, the Divine Master, it was the fault of the race."[17] For God to have been responsible for the enslavement of blacks, he would have had to control and direct history in a providential manner. It is clear that Garvey did not perceive God as the director and controller of history and human affairs.

According to Garvey, for man to know who he really is means for him to realize that he has no human master. He took the position that the only master that man had was God. Man, in terms of his rightful place in creation, was conceived by Garvey as a sovereign lord. This applies both to individual men and to races. Garvey said that this position made man courageous, bold, and impossible to enslave. What does it take then to be a man? To be a man in Garvey's eyes meant never to give up, never to depend upon others to do what one ought to do for oneself, and to

159

be one who will not blame God, nature, or fate for one's condition. But the real man, said Garvey, goes out and makes conditions to suit himself. Garvey called upon blacks to know themselves and to realize that in them is a sovereign power, an authority that is absolute.[18]

Eschatology

Marcus Garvey's eschatology was grounded first and foremost in the relentless quest for the ultimate freedom and liberation of the black race throughout the world and the acquisition of Africa as the homeland for blacks. He was not concerned with an otherworldly hope, nor did he believe that God would vindicate the black race for their sufferings. It was not his contention that God would intervene in the distant future and liberate the black race. In fact, he blatantly condemned the view held among some black leaders at the time that the problem of black and white polarization in America would work itself out and that all the black man had to do was to be humble, submissive, and obedient, and everything would work out well in the sweet bye and bye.[19] To the contrary, Garvey argued that if the black race is to be free, they must assert themselves with all their might and in every respect. They cannot depend upon God to free them, they cannot depend upon any other race for freedom, and they cannot hope for conditions to improve without human effort. But with the help of God, Garvey declared that the time had come for the black race to carve out a pathway for themselves in the course of life. He said that the black race "shall go forward, upward and onward toward the great goal of human liberty" and that it was his determination that all barriers placed in the way of the progress of the black race must be removed and cleared away by blacks themselves because the light of a brighter day had come.

160

This brighter day, as Garvey perceived it, was the eschatological vision of an independent African nationality for the black race.[20]

Contribution

There are many significant and sustaining theological motifs that emerged from Marcus Garvey and that are existentially relevant for contemporary black Americans. He did not think of God as a reality detached and removed from the black-liberation struggle. He conceived of God as a reality whose metaphysical nature made his existence an integral part of the liberation struggle. God-talk, for Garvey, emerged out of the context of existential blackness and, therefore, functioned in the interest of black Americans. Garvey did not think of God in a way that minimized the efforts of black Americans toward liberation. But rather his contention was that God was a God of power, and if blacks were to be free, they must work from the perspective of social, economic, political, educational, and religious power. He felt that God would only help black Americans achieve freedom if they would utilize all their resources to the maximum capacity. Garvey developed theology organically in light of such sustaining ideas as self-assertions, independence, self-determination, nationhood, courage, strength, love, justice, righteousness, and corporate consciousness.

In spite of the many weaknesses of the Garvey movement, we cannot overly emphasize the importance of Marcus Garvey and the Garvey movement. He saw a need within the black community and devoted his life to trying to satisfy it. He continued the great legacy of black nationalistic consciousness and the development of black pride and self-respect. Regardless of what others may do in aiding blacks in America and throughout the world toward liberation, Garvey realized that if blacks were to be truly free they must take the initiative in the process. All of Garvey's theological motifs were geared toward the actualization of the freedom and liberation of blacks throughout the world.

Conclusion

From Nathaniel Paul to Marcus Garvey the basic motif that flows throughout their respective theological systems is that of liberation. They were primarily concerned with using spirituality in the eradication of slavery and oppression in America. This process took various shapes and forms, but it never ceased to have a dominant place in their ministry. It is very clear that their hopes were not of a compensatory nature, and neither were their hopes grounded in otherworldly eschatological concerns or heavenly concerns; but, as was said earlier, their dreams were for the transformation of the social, political, and economic structures of society. Their organismic conception of reality enabled them to create a proper balance between spiritual liberation and physical liberation. They did not view man dualistically, nor did they compartmentalize the sacred and the secular. Because they viewed both man and the cosmos as consisting of a union between the spiritual and the physical, they realized that in order to make man authentic and complete, it was necessary for them to transform both spiritual and physical dimensions of existence.

Each thinker made many contributions toward the enhancement of black Americans toward freedom and liberation. Their theological systems were not removed from the struggle of black Americans, but rather they were shaped, formed, and grounded in the struggle. The social conditions of their day were affected by their understanding of God, man, sin, eschatology, repentance, redemption, salvation, and ethics. They were bold, firm, courageous, and willing to take a stand on issues that affected the black community.

The question for America is, How long will the cry for freedom and liberation have to continue before blacks are granted complete emancipation? Physical slavery has been eradicated, but other forms of slavery and oppression continue. How long will racism continue? The cry for freedom and liberation will not stop; it will just take different shapes and forms. The cry for freedom and liberation in America will not stop until the words of the prophet Amos are realized—that is, that justice shall flow down like waters and righteousness as a mighty stream. Oppression will not stop until man in America is not judged by the color of his skin but by the content of his character. It will not stop until the words of the prophet Isaiah are realized.

> Every valley shall be exalted, and every mountain and hill shall be made low: and the crooked shall be made straight, and the rough places plain: and the glory of the Lord shall be revealed, and all flesh shall see it together. (Isa. 40:4-5)

Notes

Chapter I

1. Carter G. Woodson, ed., *The Mind of the Negro as Reflected in Letters Written During the Crisis 1800–1860* (New York: Negro Universities Press, 1969), p. 163.
2. Paul, "An Address Delivered on the Celebration of the Abolition of Slavery in the State of New York, July 5, 1827," in Woodson, *Negro Orators and Their Orations* (New York: Russell & Russell, 1969), pp. 68–69.
3. Ibid., p. 69.
4. Ibid.
5. Ibid.
6. Ibid., p. 65
7. Paul, "Speech of Nathaniel Paul Delivered at the Anti-Colonization Meeting, London, 1833," in Dorothy Porter, ed., *Early Negro Writing 1760–1837* (Boston: Beacon Press, 1971), p. 288.
8. Paul, "Celebration of the Abolition of Slavery," p. 67.
9. Henry James Young, "Black Theology: Providence and Evil," *Duke Divinity School Review*, 40 (Spring, 1975), 87–88.
10. Paul, "Anti-Colonization Meeting, London, 1833," p. 286.
11. Paul, "Celebration of the Abolition of Slavery," p. 72.
12. Ibid., pp. 72–73.

Chapter II

1. Allen, *The Life Experience and Gospel Labors of the Rt. Rev. Richard Allen* (Nashville: Abingdon Press, 1960), p. 15.
2. Ibid.
3. For an elaboration of the conversion experience among slaves, see Clifton H. Johnson, ed., *God Struck Me Dead* (Philadelphia: Pilgrim Press, 1969).
4. Allen, *Life Experience and Gospel Labors*, p. 15.
5. Ibid., p. 17.
6. Allen, *Life Experience and Gospel Labors*, p. 17; see Haven P. Perkins, "Religion for Slaves: Difficulties and Methods," *Church History*, 10 (September, 1941), 244.
7. Raymond A. Bauer and Alice H. Bauer, "Day to Day Resistance to Slavery," *Journal of Negro History*, 27 (October, 1942), 339.

8. Quarles, *The Negro in the Making of America* (New York: Collier Books, 1969), p. 71.

9. Douglass, *Life and Times of Frederick Douglass: The Complete Autobiography* (New York: Crowell-Collier, 1962), p. 85.

10. Allen, *Life Experience and Gospel Labors*, p. 25.

11. Quarles, *The Making of America*, p. 99.

12. Allen, *Life Experience and Gospel Labors*, p. 26.

13. Ibid., p. 27.

14. Carter G. Woodson, *The History of the Negro Church* (Washington, D.C., Associated Pubs., 1929), pp. 75–76.

15. Allen, *Life Experience and Gospel Labors*, p. 21.

16. Ibid., p. 26.

17. Ibid., p. 28.

18. Ibid., p. 31.

19. Ibid., p. 69.

20. Ibid., pp. 69–70.

21. Ibid., p. 71.

22. Ibid., p. 71.

23. Ibid., p. 70.

24. Ibid.

Chapter III

1. Herbert Aptheker, *David Walker's Appeal: Its Setting and Its Meaning* (New York: Humanities Press, 1965), p. 41; Charles M. Wiltse, ed., *David Walker's Appeal* (New York: Hill and Wang, 1965), p vii.

2. Henry Highland Garnet, *Walker's Appeal and an Address to the Slaves of the United States of America* (New York: Arno Press and The New York Times, 1969), p. 7.

3. David Walker, "Walker's *Appeal*," in Sterling Stuckey, ed., *The Ideological Origins of Black Nationalism* (Boston: Beacon Press, 1972), p. 41.

4. Ibid., p. 55.

5. Ibid., p. 45.

6. Ibid., p. 51.

7. Ibid., p. 54.

8. Ibid., p. 58.

9. Ibid., p. 78.

10. Ibid., p. 44.

Chapter IV

1. Sterling Stuckey, ed., *The Ideological Origins of Black Nationalism* (Boston: Beacon Press, 1972), p. 58.

2. Herbert Aptheker, *Nat Turner's Slave Rebellion* (New York: Grove Press, Inc.), pp. 40–41. For further elaboration, see Albert B. Hart,

Slavery and Abolition: 1831–1841 (New York: Negro Universities Press, 1968), pp. 217–18, and Carter G. Woodson, *The Education of the Negro Prior to 1861* (New York: Arno Press, 1968), pp. 162–63.

3. Nat Turner, *Confessions of Nat Turner,* in Aptheker, *Nat Turner's Slave Rebellion,* pp. 135, 136.

4. Bennett, *Pioneers in Protest* (Baltimore: Penguin Books, 1969), p. 136.

5. Aptheker, *Nat Turner's Slave Rebellion,* p. 136.

6. Aptheker, *One Continual Cry: David Walker's Appeal to the Colored Citizens of the World, 1829–1830* (New York: Humanities Press, 1965), p. 21.

7. *Walker's Appeal,* p. 81.

8. *Turner's Confessions,* p. 137.

9. Ibid., p. 138.

10. Ibid.

11. Richard Allen, *Life Experiences and Gospel Labors of the Rt. Rev. Richard Allen* (Nashville: Abingdon Press, 1960), p. 71.

12. *Walker's Appeal,* p. 81.

Chapter V

1. Payne, *Recollections of Seventy Years* (New York: Arno Press & The New York Times, 1969), p. 15.

2. Ibid., p. 17.

3. Ibid., p. 20.

4. Ibid., p. 19.

5. Ibid., p. 27.

6. Carter G. Woodson, *The Education of the Negro Prior to 1861* (New York: Arno Press, 1968), p. 129.

7. Payne, *Recollections of Seventy Years,* p. 28.

8. Payne, "God," p. 3. Reprinted in Charles Killian, ed., *Religion in America* (New York: Arno Press, 1972).

9. Payne, "Document: Bishop Daniel Alexander Payne's Protestation of American Slavery," pp. 63–64. Reprinted in *Journal of Negro History,* January, 1967 (LII), pp. 59–64.

10. Payne, *History of the African Methodist Episcopal Church* (Nashville: A.M.E. Publication, 1891), p. viii.

11. Ibid.

12. Payne, "Protestation of American Slavery," p. 60.

13. Ibid., pp. 60, 62.

14. Ibid., p. 62.

15. Ibid.

16. Frazier and C. Eric Lincoln, *The Negro Church in America* (New York: Schocken Books, 1969), pp. 23–25.

17. Payne, "Protestation of American Slavery," p. 63.

18. Ibid.

19. Payne, *Recollection of Seventy Years,* p. 234.

20. Payne, "Protestation of American Slavery," p. 60.
21. Payne, *Recollections of Seventy Years*, p. 234.
22. Ibid., p. 207.
23. Ibid., p. 28.
24. Payne, "Protestation of American Slavery," p. 60.
25. Payne, "Protestation of American Slavery," p. 60.
26. Payne, *Recollection of Seventy Years*. From the preface by Benjamin Quarles.

Chapter VI

1. Carter G. Woodson, *History of the Negro Church* (Washington, D.C.: Associated Pubs., 1921), p. 178.
2. William Wells Brown, *The Black Man, His Antecedents, His Genius, and His Achievements* (Boston: James Redpath, 1963), p. 277.
3. Pennington, "A Lecture Delivered Before the Glasgow Y.M.C.A. and also before the St. George's Biblical Literary and Scientific Institute," London, p. 16 (found in the Fisk University Library).
4. Pennington, "A Two Year's Absence or a Farewell Sermon," p. 23 (found in the Moorland-Spingarn Collection of Howard University).
5. Ibid., pp. 23–24.
6. Pennington, "A Lecture Delivered Before the Glasgow Y.M.C.A.," p. 17.
7. Pennington, "A Two Year's Absence or Farewell Sermon," pp. 21–22.
8. Ibid., p. 22.
9. Pennington, "Christian Zeal," a sermon preached before the Third Presbytery of New York at Thirteenth St. Presbyterian Church, July 3, 1853. p. 14 (found in the Moorland-Spingarn Collection of Howard University).
10. Ibid., pp. 4, 5.
11. Pennington, "A Two Year's Absence," pp. 27–28.
12. Pennington, "A Review of Slavery and the Slave Trade," p. 156. Reprinted in the *Anglo-African Magazine* (New York: New York Times, 1969) (found in the Moorland-Spingarn Collection of Howard University).
13. Ibid., p. 19.
14. Pennington, "A Lecture Delivered Before the Glasgow Y.M.C.A.," p. 18.

Chapter VII

1. Herbert Aptheker, *One Continual Cry: David Walker's Appeal to the Colored Citizens of the World, 1829–1830* (New York: Humanities Press, 1965), pp. 38–44.
2. William Brewer, "Henry Highland Garnet," *Journal of Negro History*, 13 (January, 1928), 39.

NOTES

3. Earl Ofari, *Let Your Motto Be Resistance: The Life and Thought of Henry Highland Garnet* (Boston: Beacon Press, 1972), p. 5.

4. Ibid., p. 6; see Alexander Crummell, *Africa and America* (Springfield, Mass.: Willey and Co., 1891), pp. 280–81.

5. Brewer, "Henry Highland Garnet," p. 43.

6. For an elaboration of the concept of black unity and nationalism in the thought of David Walker and Henry Highland Garnet, see Sterling Stuckey, ed., *The Ideological Origins of Black Nationalism* (Boston: Beacon Press, 1972), pp. 1–29.

7. Howard Holman Bell, ed., *Minutes of the Proceedings of the National Negro Conventions 1830–1864* (New York: Arno Press, 1969), p. 1.

8. David Walker and Garnet, *Walker's Appeal and Garnet's Address to the Slaves of the United States of America* (New York: Arno Press, 1969), p. 90.

9. Bell, "National Negro Conventions of the Middle 1840's: Moral Suasion vs. Political Action," *Journal of Negro History*, 2:247.

10. Garnet, *Address to the Slaves of the United States of America*, p. 91.

11. Ibid.

12. Garnet, "Speech Delivered at the Seventy Anniversary of the American Anti-Slavery Society, 1840," p. 129, in Ofari, *Life and Thought of Henry Highland Garnet*, pp. 129–35.

13. Garnet, "Address to the Slaves of the United States of America," p. 92.

14. Ibid.

15. Raymond A. Bauer and Alice H. Bauer, "Day to Day Resistance to Slavery," *Journal of Negro History*, 27 (October, 1942), 417.

16. Ibid., p. 399.

17. Garnet, "Address to the Slaves of the United States of America," pp. 92–93.

18. Ibid., p. 93.

19. Ibid.

20. Ibid., p. 94.

21. Ibid.

22. Ibid.

23. Ibid.

24. Ibid.

25. Ibid. pp. 93–96.

26. Ibid.; Henry Highland Garnet, "Eulogy of John Brown," New York City, 1859, in Ofari, *Life and Thought of Henry Highland Garnet*, p. 186.

Chapter VIII

1. Ward, *Autobiography of a Fugitive Negro* (New York: Arno Press, 1968), pp. 3–19.

2. Ibid., pp. 26, 10.

3. Ibid., pp. 79–84.

4. William Wells Brown, *The Black Man, His Antecedents, His Genius, and His Achievements* (James Redpath Pub., 1863), p. 284. See also Carter G. Woodson, *History of the Negro Church* (Washington, D.C.: Associated Pubs., 1921), p. 182.

5. Ward, *Autobiography of a Fugitive Negro*, p. 43.

6. "The Dred Scott Decision, 1857," in Herbert Aptheker, ed., *A Documentary History of the Negro People in the United States: Vol. I—from Colonial Times Through the Civil War* (New York: The Citadel Press, 1969), p. 392.

7. Ibid.

8. Ward, *Autobiography of a Fugitive Negro*, pp. 37–38.

9. Ibid., pp. 40–41.

10. Ibid., pp. 63, 67, 68.

11. Ibid., p. 111.

12. Ibid., p. 69.

13. Ibid., pp. 70–75.

14. Aptheker, *Documentary History of the Negro People*, p. 299.

15. Woodson, *History of the Negro Church*, p. 183.

16. Ward, *Autobiography of a Fugitive Negro*, p. 107.

17. Ward, "Impartial Citizen," editorial reprinted in Aptheker, ed., *Documentary History of the Negro People*, p. 306.

18. McKay, "If We Must Die," in *Black Voices: An Anthology of Afro-American Literature*, ed. Abraham Chapman (New York: New American Library, 1968), pp. 372–73.

19. Ward, "Impartial Citizen," p. 306.

20. Quoted from August Meier and Elliott M. Rudwick, *From Plantation to Ghetto* (New York: Hill and Wang, 1968), p. 119.

21. Brown, *The Black Man*, p. 284.

22. Ward, *Autobiography of a Fugitive Negro*, p. 108.

Chapter IX

1. Wilson J. Moses, "Civilizing Missionary: A Study of Alexander Crummell," *The Journal of Negro History* (April, 1975), p. 233.

2. Crummell, *Africa and America* (Springfield, Mass.: Willey & Company, 1891), p. 278.

3. Ibid., pp. 279–80.

4. Ibid.

5. See the George W. Forbes Papers, Rare Book Department, Boston Public Library, pp. 5, 6.

6. Ibid., pp. 6–7.

7. Crummell, *Africa and America*, p. 414.

8. Ibid., pp. 414–15.

9. Ibid., p. 415.

10. Ibid.

11. Ibid., p. 416.

12. Ibid., p. 447.

13. Ibid., p. 418.

14. Ibid., pp. 418–19.

15. John Hope Franklin, *From Slavery to Freedom; A History of Negro Americans* (New York: Vintage Books, 1969), p. 34.

16. Crummell, *Africa and America,* pp. 418–19.

17. Ibid., p. 419

18. Ibid.

19. Ibid., p. 420.

20. From August Meier, ed., *The Making of Black America:* New York: Atheneum, 1969), p. 195.

21. Young, "Black Theology: Providence and Evil," pp. 87–96.

22. Crummell, *The Future of Africa* (New York: Charles Scribner, 1862), p. 352.

23. Crummell, "The Destined Superiority of the Negro Race," a Thanksgiving Discourse, 1877, pp. 349–52 (in *The Greatness of Christ and Other Sermons,* microfilmed, Schomburg Collection of Negro Literature and History, New York Public Library).

24. Crummell, "The Social Principle Among a People and Its Bearing on Their Progress and Development, Thanksgiving Day, 1875," see Crummell's *The Greatness of Christ and Other Sermons,* pp. 288–89.

25. Crummell, *Africa and America,* p. 41.

26. Ibid., pp. 42–49.

27. Ibid., p. 49.

28. Ibid.

29. Ibid., p. 51.

30. Ibid.

31. Ibid., p. 52.

32. Ibid., p. 449.

33. Ibid.

34. Ibid., p. 53.

35. Ibid.

36. Ibid.

37. Ibid., p. 54.

38. Crummell, "The Solution of Problems: The Duty and the Destiny of Man," pp. 10–16, microfilmed, Schomburg Collection of Negro Literature and History, New York Public Library.

39. Geroge W. Forbes Papers, pp. 9–10.

Chapter X

1. Hollis R. Lynch, *Edward Wilmot Blyden: Pan-Negro Patriot 1832–1912* (New York: Oxford University Press, 1967), pp. 3–6.

2. Lynch, ed., *Black Spokesman: Selected Published Writings of Edward Wilmot Blyden* (New York: Humanities Press, 1971), pp. xii–xv.

3. Blyden, *Christianity, Islam and the Negro Race,* ed. Christopher Fife (Edinburgh: University Press, 1967), p. 71.

4. Ibid., p. 29.

5. Ibid.

6. Ibid., p. 32.

7. Ibid.

8. Blyden, "The African Problem and the Method of Its Solution," in Howard Brotz, ed., *Negro Social and Political Thought: 1850–1920* (New York: Basic Books, 1966), p. 138.

9. Ibid.

10. Blyden, *Christianity, Islam and the Negro Race,* p. 37.

11. Blyden, "The Call of Providence to the Descendents of Africa in America," in Brotz, ed., *Negro Social and Political Thought* (New York: Basic Books, 1966), p. 114.

12. Ibid., p. 115.

13. Ibid., pp. 116–17.

14. Ibid., p. 117.

15. Blyden, "The African Problem and the Method of Its Solution," pp. 137–38.

16. Blyden, *African Life and Customs* (London: African Publication Society, 1969), p. 7.

17. Blyden, "Study and Race," in Lynch, ed., *Black Spokesman,* p. 201.

18. Ibid., pp. 201–2.

19. Blyden, "The Origin and Purpose of African Colonization," in Lynch, ed., *Black Spokesman,* pp. 39–43.

20. Blyden, *Christianity, Islam and the Negro Race,* p. 129.

Chapter XI

1. Mungo M. Ponton, *Life and Times of Henry M. Turner* (New York: Negro Universities Press, 1970), p. 33; J. Minton Batten, "Henry McNeal Turner: Negro Bishop Extraordinary," *Church History,* 7 (1938), 232–33. See also D. W. Culp, ed., *Twentieth Century Negro Literature* (Nashville, Ill., 1902), pp. 42–43; Ponton, *Life and Times of Henry M. Turner,* p. 33.

2. Batten, "Negro Bishop Extraordinary," p. 233.

3. Ponton, *Life and Times of Henry M. Turner,* pp. 34–35.

4. Batten, "Negro Bishop Extraordinary," p. 234.

5. Ibid., p. 235.

6. Josephus R. Coan, "Henry McNeal Turner: A Fearless Prophet of Black Liberation," *Journal of the Interdenominational Theological Center,* 1 (1973), 11.

7. Edwin S. Redkey, ed., *Respect Black: The Writings and Speeches of Henry McNeal Turner* (New York: Arno Press, 1971), p. 176.

8. Ibid., pp. 176, 177.

9. Ibid., p. 176.

10. Ibid., p. 74.

11. Ibid.
12. Ibid.
13. Ibid.
14. Ibid., p. 4.
15. Ibid., pp. 14, 29.
16. Redkey, "Bishop Turner's African Dream," p. 273.
17. Redkey, *Respect Black*, p. 13.
18. Ibid.
19. Ibid., pp. 13, 161.
20. Ibid., p. 170.
21. Ibid., pp. 14–15.
22. Ibid., pp. 16, 27, 168.
23. Ibid., pp. 29–30.
24. Ibid., pp. viii–ix.

Chapter XII

1. John Henrik Clarke, ed., *Marcus Garvey and the Vision of Africa* (New York: Random House, 1974), p. 29.
2. Ibid., p. 4.
3. See Hollis R. Lynch, *Introduction to the Philosophy and Opinions of Marcus Garvey*, Amy Jacques-Garvey, ed. (New York: Atheneum, 1969).
4. Garvey, *Philosophy and Opinions*, II, p. 126.
5. Ibid., pp. 126–27.
6. Ibid., pp. 128–29.
7. Ibid., p. 130.
8. Ibid., pp. 121–30.
9. Ibid., p. 122.
10. Ibid., p. 123; ibid., I, p. 73.
11. Ibid., p. 73.
12. Ibid., pp. 43–44.
13. Ibid., p. 44.
14. Ibid., p. 32.
15. Ibid.
16. Ibid.
17. Ibid., p. 37.
18. Ibid., p. 57.
19. Ibid., p. 73.
20. Ibid., pp. 70–73.